ESSENTIAL
FRENCH RIVIERA

Written and updated by Teresa Fisher

© AA Media Limited 2008
First published 2008. Reprinted 2011

ISBN: 978-0-7495-6793-4

Published by AA Publishing, a trading name of AA Media Limited, whose registered
office is Fanum House, Basing View, Basingstoke, Hampshire RG21 4EA.
Registered number 06112600.

Colour separation: MRM Graphics Ltd
Printed and bound in Italy by Printer Trento S.r.l.

A04193
Maps in this title produced from mapping © MAIRDUMONT/Falk Verlag 2011
Transport map © Communicarta Ltd, UK

About this book

Symbols are used to denote the following categories:

✚ map reference to maps on cover

✉ address or location

☎ telephone number

🕐 opening times

✋ admission charge

🍴 restaurant or café on premises
  or nearby

Ⓜ nearest underground train station

🚌 nearest bus/tram route

🚉 nearest overground train station

⛴ nearest ferry stop

✈ nearest airport

❓ other practical information

ℹ tourist information office

➤ indicates the page where you will
  find a fuller description

This book is divided into six sections.

The essence of the French Riviera
pages 6–19
Introduction; Features; Food and Drink;
Short Break including the 10 Essentials

Planning pages 20–33
Before You Go; Getting There; Getting
Around; Being There

Best places to see pages 34–55
The unmissable highlights of any visit
to the French Riviera

Best things to do pages 56–79
Great cafés; Stunning views; Places to
take the children and more

Exploring pages 80–185
The best places to visit in the French
Riviera, organized by area

Maps
All map references are to the maps on
the covers. For example, Grasse has the
reference ✚ 18K – indicating the grid
square in which it is to be found

Admission prices
Inexpensive (under €3)
Moderate (€4–€8)
Expensive (over €8)

Hotel prices
Price are per room per night:
€ inexpensive (under €80); €€ moderate
(€80–€150); €€€ expensive to luxury
(over over €150)

Restaurant prices
Price for a three-course meal per
person without drinks: € inexpensive
(under €25); €€ moderate (€25–€60);
€€€ expensive (over €60)

Contents

BEST THINGS TO DO

56 – 79

EXPLORING...

80 – 185

The essence of...

Why does the Riviera remain so popular with connoisseurs of the good things in life, and those who could afford to live and holiday anywhere in the world? Some come for the exceptionally mild winters or the grandeur of the rugged coast. Others favour the art treasures, the ancient ruins and the sleepy villages. Many more come simply for the glamour of the seaside resorts. The charms of the Riviera are so varied that most visitors are at a loss to know where to start. First-time visitors soon fall under the region's spell while those who already know it remain enchanted, returning year after year.

features

Ever since the poet Stephen Liégeard visited the Riviera in 1887 and exclaimed 'Côte d'Azur!', this dramatic stretch of azure coast with its chic resorts, fishing villages, sandy beaches, and craggy corniches has attracted a rich assortment of actors, artists, writers, film stars and royalty. For this is the home of the rich and famous, the cradle of impressionism, the home of the bikini and the world's most sophisticated holiday playground.

But what is so magical about the Riviera that it should draw millions of devotees back year after year for their annual fix of heady, Mediterranean *joie de vivre*? Is it the luxury hotels, designer shops, palm-lined promenades and terrace cafés of the exclusive resorts which bask in the scorching Mediterranean sun, with their 'see-and-be-seen' ports overflowing with millionaires' yachts; or perhaps the thrill of a casino; or the glamorous sun-soaked beaches?

The Riviera is all this and much, much more. For there is another side to the region that is easy to miss. Head inland to the hidden valleys and wild Alpine scenery, where the air is fragrant with the perfumes of Provence, to discover a great wealth of sleepy villages among countryside painted with all the vivid colours of Picasso, Renoir and Matisse.

HERBES DE PROVENCE

LANGUAGE
● In some tourist centres, English threatens to become the lingua franca while a revival of traditional Provençal language – langue d'oc – is taking place in the hinterland.

LOCATION
● The Riviera, from Menton on the Italian border to le Lavandou, is squeezed onto a narrow strip of coastland between the Mediterranean and the Alpes-Maritimes.

ECONOMY
● Nice is the capital of the Alpes-Maritimes département, and its airport is the second busiest in France.
● Thanks to popular resorts such as Cannes and St-Tropez, tourism is the region's main moneymaker.
● Monaco is a world-famous financial centre and tax haven.
● North of Cannes, France's 'Silicon Valley' – the Sophia-Antipolis business park – is regarded as the technological heart of southern Europe, containing over 1,000 enterprises.

THE PRINCIPALITY OF MONACO
● Size – 195ha (482acres), including 31ha (76 acres) reclaimed from the sea.
● Population – 32,000 (including 7,000 Monégasques).
● Currency – Euro.
● Religion – Catholicism.
● National Holiday – 19 November.
● Access – 22km (14 miles) from Nice-Côte d'Azur Airport.
● Constitution – Hereditary monarchy with the Prince as Head of State. The current ruler is His Serene Highness Prince Albert II.

food & drink

France is universally recognized as the world leader in the field of food and wine, and of all its great regional styles *la cuisine Provençale* has one of the strongest personalities – piquant, aromatic Mediterranean dishes with bold, sun-drenched colours and strong earthy flavours as varied as its landscapes.

PROVENÇAL SPECIALITIES

Most Provençal dishes rely heavily on garlic, tomatoes, olive oil, onions and wild herbs (thyme, rosemary, sage and basil). Specialties include *soupe au pistou* (vegetable soup with cheese, garlic and basil; *beignets de courgettes* (zucchini flowers dipped in batter and deep fried), *mesclun* (salad leaves including dandelion and hedge-mustard), *daube* (beef stew with wine, cinnamon and lemon peel), *salade Niçoise* (with tuna, egg, black olives and anchovies) and *pain bagnat* (Niçoise salad inside a loaf of bread).

The Riviera is a region of olive groves. The local black or green olives

make tasty *tapenades* (olive pastes with capers and anchovies), delicious served on crusty bread with sun-dried tomatoes. Other local delicacies include truffles, lavender-scented honey and a medley of tasty mountain cheeses. Near the coast, fish dishes reign supreme. Expect to pay at least €45 for a decent *bouillabaisse*, or try *bourride* – poor man's fish soup! *Moules frites* (mussels with french fries) are always good value, and don't be surprised if you are presented with a plate of shiny, black, seaweed-draped *oursin* (sea urchins) as they are considered a great delicacy. Simply scrape out the rosy-pink insides and eat them raw with a glass of chilled white wine.

CUISINE NIÇOISE

The Nice area has developed its own distinctive 'Nissart' cuisine within the Provençal tradition. It reflects the town's former association with Italy, with dishes that seductively blend the best of French and Italian traditions. Indeed, pizzas and pastas taste every

bit as good in Menton and Nice as they do over the border, and you have never really had ravioli until you try a plateful in Nice, where the dish was first invented. Look also for *pissaladière* (olive and onion pizza), *socca* (thin pancakes made of chickpea flour), *petits farcis* (savoury stuffed artichoke hearts, courgettes and tomatoes) and *estocaficada* (stockfish stew).

LOCAL WINES

Eleven per cent of France's wine comes from Provence. The chalky soil and warm, dry, Mediterranean climate lend themselves to the development of smooth, easy-to-drink wines such

as Côtes de Provence, known mainly for its dry, fruity, rosé wines. For the adventurous wine drinker there are several wines in the AOC (Appellation d'Origine Contrôlée) category, which come mainly from areas just to the west of the Riviera, but which can readily be found on restaurant wine lists. Particularly sought-after (and not usually cheap) wines include the vigorous red Bandol, the dry white Cassis, and reds, rosés and whites from Palette. The tiny wine region of Bellet near Nice produces some particularly fragrant and full-bodied reds, whites and rosés. The locals swear these wines are the best accompaniments to regional dishes, but few bottles ever get beyond the cellars of the Riviera's most exclusive restaurants.

SWEETMEATS

For those with a sweet tooth, this sunny region produces plenty of juicy, fragrant fruits, including figs, cherries, melons, pears, strawberries and peaches. Other treats include *pain d'épice* (spiced bread), delicious *marrons glacés* (crystalized chestnuts) from Collobrières, tempting nougat from St-Tropez, and caramelized figs from Grasse.

short break

If you have only a short time to visit the Riviera, or would like to get a really complete picture of the region, here are the essentials:

● **Bask in the sun on one of the Riviera's sandy beaches,** or relax under the shade of a classic striped parasol.

● **Visit the cours Saleya market in Nice** (➤ 88), and treat yourself to a picnic of goat's cheese, tomatoes, olives and local wine.

● **Promenade the waterfront at St-Tropez** (➤ 164) in your finery, admiring its ostentatious yachts and gin palaces (…and don't forget your designer sunglasses!).

● **Visit some of France's finest modern art galleries:** Fondation Maeght (➤ 42), Musée Matisse (➤ 48), Musée Picasso (➤ 52), Musée Renoir (➤ 117), Musée de l'Annonciade (➤ 167).

● **Dine in one of Mougins' world-class restaurants** (➤ 58), and marvel at the enticing tastes, fragrances and colours of Provençal cuisine.

● **Try a little gambling** at the world-famous Casino de Monte-Carlo (➤ 36).

● **Join the laid-back locals in a game of** *boules* – this ancient game originated here and, although now played throughout the world, the most fiercely contested games still take place in the shady village squares of the French Riviera.

● **Spot the rich and famous at the Cannes Film Festival,** the glitziest, most glamorous event on the Côte d'Azur.

● **Escape the frenetic coastal resorts** and explore the sleepy surrounding countryside, dotted with hilltop villages.

● **Create your very own scent** at one of Grasse's many perfumeries (➤ 122).

Planning

Before you go

WHEN TO GO

JAN	FEB	MAR	APR	MAY	JUN	JUL	AUG	SEP	OCT	NOV	DEC
12°C	12°C	14°C	18°C	21°C	27°C	28°C	28°C	25°C	22°C	17°C	14°C
54°F	54°F	57°F	64°F	70°F	81°F	82°F	82°F	77°F	72°F	63°F	57°F

🌨️ 🌨️ 🌨️ ☀️ ☀️ ☀️ ☀️ ☀️ ☁️ ☁️ 🌨️ 🌨️

🔴 High season ⚪ Low season

The climate in the French Riviera is typically Mediterranean, with approximately 300 days of sunshine a year. The best times to visit are May, June and September, avoiding the crowds of July and August. Although originally a winter resort, when visitors could enjoy the relatively mild and temperate weather, it can get cold and wet during these months, with snow in the Alps and a biting mistral wind of up to 290kph (180mph).

WHAT YOU NEED

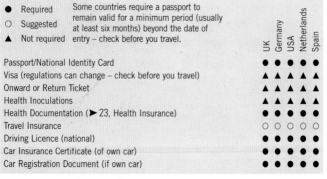

			UK	Germany	USA	Netherlands	Spain
●	Required	Some countries require a passport to remain valid for a minimum period (usually at least six months) beyond the date of entry – check before you travel.					
○	Suggested						
▲	Not required						
Passport/National Identity Card			●	●	●	●	●
Visa (regulations can change – check before you travel)			▲	▲	▲	▲	▲
Onward or Return Ticket			▲	▲	▲	▲	▲
Health Inoculations			▲	▲	▲	▲	▲
Health Documentation (▶ 23, Health Insurance)			●	●	●	●	●
Travel Insurance			○	○	○	○	○
Driving Licence (national)			●	●	●	●	●
Car Insurance Certificate (of own car)			●	●	●	●	●
Car Registration Document (if own car)			●	●	●	●	●

WEBSITES

www.guideriviera.com
www.nicetourism.com
www.francetourism.com

www.ot-saint-tropez.com
www.cannes-on-line.com
www.visitmonaco.com

TOURIST OFFICES AT HOME

In the UK

French Government Tourist Office
178 Piccadilly
London W1J 9AL
☎ 09068 244123
(recorded information)

Maison de Monaco à Londres
7 Upper Grosvenor Street
Mayfair
London
W1K 2LX
☎ 020 74914264

In the USA

French Government Tourist Office
444 Madison Avenue, 16th floor
New York
NY 10022
☎ 212/286-8310

Monaco Government Tourist
Bureau
565 Fifth Avenue, 23rd floor
New York
NY10017
☎ 800/753-9696

HEALTH INSURANCE

Nationals of EU countries can obtain medical treatment at reduced cost with the relevant documentation (EHIC – European Health Insurance Card), although private medical insurance is still advised and is essential for all other visitors.

As for general dental treatment, nationals of EU countries can obtain dental care at reduced cost with an EHIC. Around 70 per cent of dentists' standard fees are refundable. Private medical insurance is still advisable for all. US visitors should check their insurance coverage.

TIME DIFFERENCES

| GMT | France | Germany | USA (NY) | Netherlands | Spain |
| 12 noon | 1PM | 1PM | 7AM | 1PM | 1PM |

France is one hour ahead of Greenwich Mean Time (GMT+1), but from late March, when clocks are put forward one hour, until late October, French summer time (GMT+2) operates.

NATIONAL HOLIDAYS

1 Jan *New Year's Day*

27 Jan *Ste-Dévote's Day (Monaco only)*

Mar/Apr *Easter Sunday and Monday*

1 May *Labour Day*

8 May *VE Day (France only)*

May/Jun *Whit Sunday and Monday*

Jun *Corpus Christi (Monaco only)*

14 Jul *Bastille Day (France only)*

15 Aug *Assumption*

1 Nov *All Saints' Day*

11 Nov *Remembrance Day (France only)*

19 Nov *Monaco National Holiday (Monaco only)*

9 Dec *Immaculate Conception (Monaco only)*

25 Dec *Christmas Day*

WHAT'S ON WHEN

January *Fête de Ste-Dévote*, Monaco

Monte-Carlo Car Rally (end of month)

Monte-Carlo International Circus Festival (third week)

February *Nice Carnival* (two weeks)

Fête du Citron, Menton (10-day festival ➤ 151)

Corso du Mimosa, Bormes-les-Mimosas (10 Feb, ➤ 171)

Olive and Grape Festival, Valbonne

March *Dance Festival*, Cannes

Festin es Courgourdons – festival of dried, sculpted gourds, Nice

Fête des Violettes, Tourrettes-sur-Loup (➤ 128)

Semi Marathon International de Nice

April *International Tennis Open*, Nice and Monaco

Ski Grand Prix, Isola 2000

Procession of the Dead Christ, Roquebrune-Cap-Martin (Maundy Thursday/Good Friday)

May *Cannes Film Festival* (2nd week ➤ 62, 121)

Fête de la Rose, Grasse (2nd weekend)

Bravade de Saint-Torpes, St-Tropez (16–18 May ➤ 167)

International Formula One Grand Prix, Monaco

June *Sacred Music Festival*, Nice

Procession dai Limaça – snail Festival, Gorbio

Bravade des Espagnols, St-Tropez (15 Jun)

July *Nice Jazz Festival* (first two weeks)

International Art Festival, Cagnes

Nikaïa – International Athletics Meeting, Nice
Fête Nationale – Bastille Day fête with fireworks, Nice (14 Jul)
Fête de Saint-Pierre, with water jousting, Cap d'Antibes (second Sunday)
Modern Music Festival, St-Paul-de-Vence (Jul–Aug)
Summer Jazz Festival, Juan-les-Pins (two weeks)
International Fireworks Festival, Monaco (Jul–Aug)
Numerous arts festivals at Beaulieu-sur-Mer, Menton, St-Paul-de-Vence,
Vence and other towns and villages
August *Jazz and Theatre Festival*, Ramatuelle (➤ 177)
Chamber Music Festival, Menton
Jasmine Festival, Grasse (first Sun)
Passion Procession, Roquebrune (5 Aug)
Pays de Fayence Music Festival (➤ 121)
September *Festin des Baguettes*, Peille
Triathlon de Nice
Les Voiles de St-Tropez Yacht Regatta (end Sep–1st week Oct)
October *Provençal Daly*, Valbonne
November *Expo-Cannes* (Nov/Dec)
December *Bain de Noël* – skinny-dipping in the Med (first Sun
after Christmas)

Getting there

BY AIR

Nice-Côte d'Azur Airport

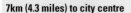

7km (4.3 miles) to city centre

N/A

20 minutes

15 minutes

Nice's airport, Aéroport Nice Côte d'Azur (☎ 08 20 42 33 33 within France or ☎ 04 89 88 98 28 from abroad; www.nice.aeroport.fr), is situated just 7km (4.3 miles) to the west of Nice city centre. It ranks top among French airports after Paris with nearly ten million passengers a year. The airport has two terminals, with a free shuttle bus between the two. International flights use both terminals, while most domestic flights use terminal two.

The national airline, Air France (☎ 08 02 82 08 20 in France) has scheduled flights to Nice-Côte d'Azur Airport from Britain, mainland Europe and beyond. The airport is increasingly well-served by low-cost airlines from various UK and European destinations. The best deals can be found by booking well in advance through the websites of leading airlines and tour operators. The flight time from London is approximately two hours. Visitors from the USA can fly directly with Air France into Paris or one of the other main European hubs, then take a connecting flight to Nice.

Airport facilities are excellent and include numerous shops, restaurants, bars, banks, a bureaux de change, ATMs, a post office, a chemist, car rental facilities and a dedicated business centre.

The best way to reach the city centre from the airport is by taxi. This takes around 10–20 minutes depending on the time of day, but it is the most expensive option. There is also a regular bus service every 20 minutes (6:10am–8:55pm) from the airport to Nice's *Gare Routière* (main bus station). Purchase your ticket from the driver of the bus. There are also regular buses to Cannes, Monaco and Menton. Alternatively, travel in style with frequent helicopter transits from Nice Côte d'Azur airport to Monte-Carlo, Cannes and St-Tropez.

BY RAIL

SNCF, the French rail network, links the main stations along the Riviera to major cities throughout France and abroad, including a high speed train link (Trains à Grande Vitesse or TGV) directly from Paris Gare de Lyon, which takes six hours to Nice. Seat reservations are required on all TGV trains. For further information contact SNCF (www.sncf.com) and Rail Europe (www.raileurope.com).

BY ROAD

A major road network of fast, efficient autoroutes (motorways) links the French Riviera to Paris, Italy, Spain and northern Europe. The quickest route south through France is the Autoroute du Soleil, the A6 autoroute from Paris to Lyon, followed by the A7 to Marseille, and then the A8 to Nice and on to Italy. From Spain, the A9 autoroute leads from Barcelona to join the A8 at Orange. For the ambitious or the unrushed, an alternative route – La Route Napoléon – winds from Grenoble southward across the Alps to Digne and then on to Grasse. From Grasse, take the picturesque D3 down to the coast at Cannes, or the D2210 to Nice.

Before you leave home, make sure you have the appropriate insurance (➤ 22), and remember that the headlights of right-hand drive cars must be adjusted before you drive in mainland Europe. It is advisable to plan your route in advance with a detailed map. Remember to drive on the right, wear your seatbelt at all times and stick to the speed limits (➤ 29). When you join an autoroute, collect a ticket from the machine which indicates your start-point. You do not need to pay again until you reach an exit toll, where you will be charged for the distance travelled and for your vehicle type. You can pay with cash or by credit card. The A8 is the most expensive stretch of toll autoroute in France.

If you don't fancy driving, Eurolines offers a comprehensive long-distance bus network across Europe. See their website (www.eurolines.com) for further information.

BY SEA

The Mediterranean is famous as a popular cruising destination and various companies operate to the Riviera, stopping at St-Tropez, Villefranche and Monaco. There are also regular ferries from Nice to Corsica.

Getting around

PUBLIC TRANSPORT

Internal flights Air France links 45 cities and towns, including Nice, Cannes and Fréjus.

Trains The main line of the Riviera links the main towns and cities with the Rhône Valley. A spectacular stretch runs along the coast from Fréjus/ St-Raphaël to Menton, which in summer is the most efficient way to travel along this busy stretch of coastline.

Area buses Services run by a number of private companies are punctual and comfortable, but not very frequent outside main urban areas and coastal resorts. There are also SNCF buses, which serve places on rail routes where trains do not stop. For further information, contact Nice bus station (☎ 04 93 85 61 81).

Island ferries One of the best ways to explore the Riviera's coastline is by boat. There are frequent ferries to the nearby Îles de Lérins from Cannes, a coastal service between le Lavandou, Cavalaire-sur-Mer,

St-Tropez and Ste-Maxime in summer (contact local tourist offices for details), and daily sailings to Corsica from the Vieux Port (Old Port) of Nice.

Urban transport Most sizeable towns have a bus station *(gare routière)*, often near the railway station. Services, even in cities, stop about 9pm. The most efficient bus network is in Nice, where computerised boards at every bus stop inform you of the exact time of arrival of your service.

Tram nice Nice is currently building a new tram line. At the time of writing three routes were planned with the first one due for completion sometime in 2007. The U-shaped route will pass through the centre and serve the city's northern and eastern suburbs. It will cost the same as the bus and will operate every 15 minutes (every 4 minutes during rush hour) from 5am–1am.

TAXIS

Taxis are very expensive and not allowed to cruise. They must pick up at ranks *(stations de taxi)* found at airports, railway stations and elsewhere. Always be sure there is a meter. There is a pick-up charge plus a rate per minute – check with the driver.

DRIVING

- The French drive on the right side of the road.
- Seatbelts must be worn in front seats at all times and in rear seats where fitted.
- Random breath-testing takes place. Never drive under the influence of alcohol.
- Petrol *(essence)* including unleaded *(sans plomb)* is widely available. Petrol stations are numerous along main roads but rarer in mountainous areas. Some on minor roads are closed on Sunday. Most take credit cards. Maps showing fuel stations are available from main tourist offices.
- Speed limits are as follows:
  Autoroutes (motorways/highways): 130kph (80mph)
  Dual carriageways: 110kph (70mph)
  Main roads: 90kph (55mph)
  Minor roads: 50kph (30mph)
- A red warning triangle must by carried if your car has no hazard warning lights, but it is advised for all motorists. Place this 30m (98ft) behind the car in the event of an accident or breakdown. On autoroutes ring from emergency phones (every 2km/1.2 miles) to contact the local breakdown service. Off autoroutes, police will advise on local services.

CAR RENTAL

Major car-rental companies have desks at Nice-Côte d'Azur Airport and in the main towns. Car rental is expensive, but airlines and tour operators offer fly-drive, and French Railways (SNCF) train/car packages, which are often more economical.

Being there

TOURIST OFFICES
Regional office
- Comité Régional de
  Tourisme Riviera Côte d'Azur
  400 promenade des Anglais
  BP 602
  06011 Nice
  ☎ 04 93 37 78 78

Local tourist offices
- Syndicat d'Initiative
  Palais des Festivals
  1a La Croisette
  Esplanade du Président-Georges
  Pompidou, Cannes
  ☎ 04 93 99 84 22
- Office du Tourisme et des
  Congrès, 5 promenade des
  Anglais, Nice
  ☎ 0892 707 407

- Office National du Tourisme de la
  Principauté de Monaco
  2a boulevard des Moulins
  Monte-Carlo
  MC 98030 Monaco
  ☎ 377/92 16 61 16
- Office du Tourisme
  quai Jean Jaurès
  BP 183
  83990 St-Tropez
  ☎ 04 94 97 45 21

MONEY
The euro is the official currency of France and Monaco. Banknotes are in denominations of 5, 10, 20, 50, 100, 200 and 500 euros and coins are in denominations of 1, 2, 5, 10, 20 and 50 cents, and 1 and 2 euros. Euro travellers' cheques are widely accepted as are major credit cards. Credit and debit cards can also be used for withdrawing cash from ATMs.

TIPS/GRATUITIES

Yes ✓ No ✗		
Restaurants/cafés/bars	✓	15% if service not incl.
Tour guides	✓	€3–5
Hotels (service incl; tip optional)	✓	€1.50 per bag/day
Taxis	✓	10%

POSTAL SERVICES

The PTT (*Poste et Télécommunications*) deals with mail and telephone services. Offices open from 8am–7pm (noon Sat, closed Sun).

Outside main centres, post offices open shorter hours and may close between noon and 2pm. Letter boxes are yellow.

☎ 04 93 82 65 00 (Nice) ☎ 377/97 97 25 25 (Monaco)

TELEPHONES

All telephone numbers in France have ten digits (eight in Monaco). There are no area codes except for Monaco (377 precedes the number when phoning from outside the principality). Phone cards *(télécartes)* are sold in post offices, tobacconists and newsagents. The code for France is 33.

International dialling codes

From France and Monaco dial 00
followed by
UK: 44
Germany: 49
USA / Canada: 1
Netherlands: 31
Spain: 34

Emergency telephone numbers

Police: 17
Fire: 18
Ambulance: 15

EMBASSIES AND CONSULATES

UK ☎ 04 93 62 13 56 (N)
377/93 50 99 54 (M)
Germany ☎ 04 93 83 55 25 (N)
377/97 77 51 53 (M)
USA ☎ 04 93 88 89 55 (N)

Netherlands ☎ 04 93 87 52 94 (N)
377/ 92 05 15 02 (M)
Spain ☎ 377/93 30 24 98 (M)

Key: (N) – Nice; (M) – Monaco

HEALTH ADVICE

Sun advice The sunniest (and hottest) months are July and August with an average of 10 hours sun a day and daytime temperatures of 28°C (82°F). Particularly during these months you should avoid the midday sun and use a strong sunblock. Drink plenty of water during hot weather.

Drugs Pharmacies – recognized by their green cross sign – possess highly qualified staff able to offer medical advice, provide first aid and dispense prescription *(ordonnance)* drugs.

Safe water It is safe to drink tap water served in hotels and restaurants, but never drink from a tap marked *eau non potable*. Many people prefer the taste of bottled water which is cheap and readily available.

PERSONAL SAFETY

The *Police Municipale* (blue uniforms) perform police duties in cities and towns. The *Gendarmes* (blue trousers, black jackets, white belts), the national police force, cover the countryside and smaller places. The *CRS* deal with emergencies and also provide safety on beaches. Monaco has its own police. To help prevent crime:

- Do not carry more cash than you need.
- Do not leave valuables on the beach or poolside.
- Beware of pickpockets in crowded places.
- Avoid walking alone in dark alleys at night.
- Cars should be locked.

ELECTRICITY

The power supply in France is 220 volts with sockets taking two-round-pin (or occasionally three-round-pin) plugs. British visitors should bring an adaptor; US visitors need a voltage transformer.

OPENING HOURS

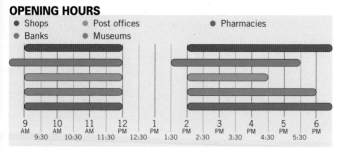

In addition to the times shown above, afternoon opening times of shops in summer can be 3–8 or 9pm. Most shops close on Sunday and many on Monday. Large department stores do not close for lunch and hypermarkets open 10–9 or 10–10 but may shut on Monday morning. Banks are closed on Sunday as well as Saturday or Monday. Some museums have extended summer hours, many close on one day a week.

LANGUAGE

French is the native language. In Monaco the traditional Monégasque language (a mixture of French, Provençal and Italian Ligurian) is spoken by the older generation. English is spoken by those involved in the tourist trade and in the larger cosmopolitan centres. However, attempts to speak French will always be appreciated. Below is a list of a few helpful words.

please	*s'il vous plaît*	how are you?	*comment ça va?*
thank you	*merci*	do you speak English?	*parlez-vous Anglais?*
hello	*bonjour*		
goodbye	*au revoir*	I don't understand	*je ne comprends pas*
good evening	*bon soir*	how much?	*combien?*
goodnight	*bonne nuit*	open/closed	*ouvert/fermé*
sorry	*pardon*	today	*aujourd'hui*
excuse me	*excusez moi*	tomorrow	*demain*
hotel room	*la chambre*	one/two night(s)	*une/deux nuit(s)*
single (room)	*une personne*	breakfast	*le petit déjeuner*
double (room)	*deux personnes*	bathroom	*la salle de bain*
per person	*par personne*	toilet	*les toilettes*
bank	*la banque*	banknote	*le billet*
exchange office	*le bureau de change*	travellers' cheque	*le chèque de voyage*
post office	*la poste*	credit card	*la carte de crédit*
coin	*la pièce*	change	*la monnaie*
lunch	*le déjeuner*	bill	*l'addition*
dinner	*le dîner*	drink	*la boisson*
table	*la table*	beer	*la bière*
waiter/waitress	*le garçon/la serveuse*	wine	*le vin*
water	*l'eau*	coffee	*le café*
airport	*l'aéroport*	single/return	*simple/retour*
train	*le train*	car	*la voiture*
bus	*l'autobus*	petrol/gasoline	*l'essence*
station	*la gare*	bus stop	*l'arrêt d'autobus*
ticket	*le billet*	where is...?	*où est...?*

Best places to see

1 Casino, Monte-Carlo

www.casinomontecarlo.com

The world's most famous casino symbolizes all that is opulent and glamorous in Monte-Carlo – a 'must-see', even if you are not a gambler.

The Casino de Monte-Carlo is probably the most famous building on the French Riviera, known in its heyday as the 'Cathedral of Hell'. It was opened in 1878 by Prince Charles III (after whom Monte-Carlo is named), to save himself from bankruptcy. Such was its success that, five years later, he abolished taxation.

The resplendent building was designed by Charles Garnier, architect of the Paris Opéra. Its lavish belle époque interior is a riot of pink, green and gold, with marble floors, bronze sculptures, onyx columns and highly ornate ceilings lit by crystal chandeliers. It was here in 1891 that Charles Deville Wells turned $400 into $40,000 in a three-day gambling spree, thus inspiring the popular tune 'The Man Who Broke the Bank at Monte-Carlo'.

Ever since gamblers have come here from all over the world to try their luck at the gaming tables. Yet gone are the days when the Monégasques could live entirely off the folly of others. Revenue from the Casino has declined, so that now it is worth much more as a tourist attraction.

The Casino building also houses the Salle Garnier, a small, highly ornate opera house (➤ 63), which, for more than a century, has welcomed the world's greatest artists.

➕ 22L ✉ place du Casino ☎ 377/92 16 20 00 🕐 Casino: daily from noon (except 1 May). European (rules) rooms from 4pm; American (rules) rooms from 5pm. Salle Garnier: open for performances (➤ 63) 💰 Expensive 🍴 Bar and restaurants (€€€) 🚌 Monaco/Monte-Carlo ❓ No persons under 18. Passport required. Jacket and tie recommended

2 Corniche de l'Esterel

Edging a wild group of blood-red porphyry mountains, the 'golden coast road' passes some of the Riviera's most grandiose scenery.

The Corniche de l'Esterel follows the dramatic shoreline from St-Raphaël to Théoule-sur-Mer, along the sole stretch of Riviera coastline that is still virtually untouched by property development. The tortuous road is punctuated by viewpoints overlooking inviting beaches, sheltered yacht harbours, jagged inlets and deserted coves cut by rocky promontories. The Massif de l'Esterel provides a perfect backdrop, with its harsh, rugged mountains of brilliant red volcanic rock jutting out into the sea.

Travelling from east to west, start at Théoule-sur-Mer, a small seaside resort at the rim of the Parc Forestier de la Pointe de l'Aiguille, an extensive coastal park offering a variety of scenic walking trails. There are plenty of hiking possibilities into the Massif de l'Esterel from the coast road. A quick climb along the Pointe de l'Esquillon at Miramar is rewarded by spectacular views of Cap Roux further along the coast.

Le Trayas is located at the highest point of the Corniche. Just beyond, a strenuous inland trail climbs the Pic du Cap Roux. The road continues to twist and turn westward via Anthéor and Agay to St-Raphaël; the Esterel's main resort which is beautifully situated around a deep horseshoe bay and considered one of the best anchorages on this stretch of coast.

Heading inland from Fréjus, the N7 road to Cannes follows the path of the Roman Via Aurelia through extensive cork forests past Mont Vinaigre (614m/2014ft), the highest peak in the Esterel. A short path leads to its summit, for an overview of the wilderness that for centuries was a popular haunt of brigands and a refuge for hermits and escaped galley-slaves from Toulon.

✚ 18G ❓ Trains run hourly from Cannes to St-Raphaël daily. Check timetables for details
🛈 Mandelieu: avenue de Cannes ☎ 04 92 97 99 27 🛈 St-Raphaël: 99 Quai Albert 1er ☎ 04 94 19 52 52

3 Èze

Without doubt one of the Riviera's most strikingly situated and best-preserved hilltop villages, Èze affords truly breathtaking views.

Èze is frequently called the Nid d'Aigle (Eagle's Nest) because of its remarkable location, perched at the summit of a rocky outcrop, halfway between Nice and Monaco, where the mountains meet the coast.

The settlement records of Èze date back as far as the 11th century although the site has been occupied since the Bronze Age. The village was fortified in the 12th century and belonged to the Counts of Savoy for hundreds of years. In 1792, following the creation of the Alpes-Maritimes, Èze became part of the Principality of Monaco. It was only after

the plebiscite of 1860, when locals voted in the village chapel for annexation to France, that peace finally came to Èze.

On entering through the only gateway in the ancient ramparts, you will be struck by the tall, golden houses and the labyrinth of tiny vaulted passages with cobbled alleys, which climb steeply up to the ruins of a once massive Saracen fortress 429m (1407ft) above sea level. It is surrounded by an **exotic garden,** bristling with magnificent cacti, succulents and rare palms.

Be sure to take time to explore the small and elegant flower-filled passageways, crammed with countless craft shops hidden in caves within the rock – tiny treasure troves of antiques, ceramics, pewter and olivewood. At the foot of the hill, two Grassois perfume factories, Galimard and Fragonard, contain interesting museums in which the secrets of perfume production are explained. Nearby, the Chemin de Nietzsche (a narrow path once frequented by the German philosopher) zigzags steeply down to the beach and the former fishing village of Èze-Bord-de-Mer, now a popular coastal resort.

✚ 22K

ℹ️ Èze: place de Gaulle ☎ 04 93 41 26 00

Jardin Exotique

✉️ rue du Château ☎ 04 93 41 10 30 🕐 Winter daily 9–dusk; Sep–Jun daily 9–6 or 7 ✋ Moderate

4 Fondation Maeght, St-Paul-de-Vence

www.fondation-maeght.com

Hidden amid umbrella pines above the village of St-Paul-de-Vence, this is one of the world's most distinguished modern art museums.

The Maeght Foundation is no ordinary museum. At its inauguration in 1964, André Malraux, Minister of Cultural Affairs, described it as 'a world in which modern art can both find its place and that otherworldliness which used to be called supernatural'.

The foundation was the brainchild of Aimé and Marguerite Maeght, who were art dealers and close friends of many artists, including Matisse, Miró, Braque, Bonnard and Chagall, and it was their private collection that formed the basis of the museum. Their aim was to create a living home for creation with accommodation for artists, and the ideal environment in which to display contemporary art. To achieve this, they worked in close collaboration with Catalan architect José-Luis Sert, a former pupil of Le Corbusier.

The resulting buildings blend artfully into the natural surroundings, respecting the curves of the landscape, and incorporating

beautiful terraces, gardens and ponds where contemporary artists have given free rein to their inspiration. Look for Miró's *Labyrinthe* – a fantastic multi-level maze of mosaics, sculptures, fountains, trees and ceramics; Chagall's vast, joyful canvas *La Vie*; and Cour Giacometti – a tiled courtyard peopled with skinny Giacometti figures. There is also a chapel on the grounds, built in memory of the Maeghts' son who died in 1953 at age 11, which contains striking stained-glass windows by Braque and Ubac.

Inside the museum, the remarkable permanent collection consists exclusively of 20th-century art and includes works by nearly every major artist of the past 50 years; these are displayed on a rotation basis throughout the year, except during summer, when temporary exhibitions are held.

✚ 20K ✉ 06570 St-Paul-de-Vence ☎ 04 93 32 81 63
🕐 Oct–Jun 10–12:30, 2:30–6; Jul–Sep 10–7 💰 Expensive
🍴 Café (€) ❓ Gift shop and art library
ℹ St-Paul-de-Vence: Maison de la tour, 2 rue Grande
☎ 04 93 32 86 95

5 Îles de Lérins

Take refuge from crowded Cannes on these two tiny islands, perfect for a stroll, a swim and a picnic, or to visit their important religious sites.

The charming, car-free Îles de Lérins lie just 20 minutes by ferry from Cannes. They are named after two saints – Saint Honorat, who founded a monastery on the smaller of the two islands at the end of the 4th century, and his sister Sainte Marguerite, who set up a nunnery on the other island – and were once the most powerful ecclesiastical centres in the south of France.

Île Ste-Marguerite is the larger of the islands. Its main attraction is undoubtedly the **Fort Royal,** which contains the Musée de la Mer (Maritime Museum), with Ligurian, Greek and Roman artefacts excavated on the island alongside objects recovered from ships sunk off its shores.

The fort was built under Richelieu, strengthened by Vauban in 1712, then restored under Napoléon. Used as a prison from 1685 until the early 20th century, its most illustrious occupant (from 1687 to 1698) was the mysterious 'Man in the Iron Mask' whose identity is still unknown.

Île St-Honorat maintains an active monastery. The 19th-century Abbaye de Lérins (www.abbayedelerins.com) is open daily to visitors, and the Cistercian monks produce lavender, oranges, honey and a sweet liqueur, made from aromatic Provençal plants.

Both islands offer pleasant walking trails. One of the most enjoyable is a shaded route around Île St-Honorat, past the seven chapels scattered across the island.

✚ 19H ⬛ Trans-Côte Azur ☎ 04 92 98 71 30; www.trans-cote-azur.com Regular crossings from Cannes' Care Maritimes ⬛ Planaria ☎ 04 92 98 71 38 Regular crossings to St-Honorat (20-mins trip) 🍴 Ferry ticket expensive ℹ Cannes: Esplanade George Pompidou ☎ 04 93 99 84 22

Fort Royal

✉ Île Ste-Marguerite ☎ 04 93 43 18 17 🕐 Closed Mon 🍴 Inexpensive

6 MAMAC, Nice

www.mamac-nice.org

The remarkable Musée d'Art Moderne et d'Art Contemporain traces the history of French and American avant-garde from the 1960s.

MAMAC was inaugurated in 1990 as a vast monument to the ambitions of the city's former National Front leader, Jacques Médecin. Even the building, designed by Yves Bayard and Henri Vidal, is a masterpiece of modern art with its four octagonal, grey-marble towers linked together by glassed-in walkways.

MAMAC's collections are exhibited in rotation and reflect the main avant-garde art movements of the last 40 years in France and the US. The primary focus is on French neo-realism and the artists of the second École de Nice, featuring works by Rayasse, César, Arman, Ben, Tinguely, and Yves Klein. Many of their works involve smashing, tearing, burning or distorting mundane objects of everyday life as a spoof on society and the highbrow art world.

Look for artists of the *support-surface* movement (who sought to reduce painting to its materialistic reality, concentrating on the frame and the texture of the canvas) and the graffiti-obsesssed 'Fluxus' movement, best portrayed in the fun, push-button Little Shop of Ben. American abstraction, minimalism and pop art are also well represented. Highlights include several Lichtenstein cartoons and one of Warhol's famous Campbell's soup tin pieces.

No visit to MAMAC would be complete without visiting the rooftop terraces for unsurpassed views of Nice. Here, on special occasions, the illumination of Klein's *Mur de Feu* (Wall of Fire) is a unique spectacle.

✚ *Nice 6c* ✉ promenade des Arts
☎ 04 97 13 42 01 🕐 Daily 10–6. Closed Mon and hols 👜 Moderate 🍴 Café and restaurant (€€) 🚌 3, 4, 5, 6, 7, 9, 10, 14 16, 17, 25, 30 🚊 Nice ❓ Gift shop. Auditorium showing art videos

7

Musée Matisse, Nice

Here in this handsome villa is a remarkable collection – a visual history of Matisse's works that spans his entire life and should appeal to everyone.

Henri Matisse came to live in Nice in 1917 and, shortly before his death in 1954, he bequeathed his entire personal collection to the city. Together with a second, even bigger, donation from his wife in 1960 (including over 100 personal effects from his studio in the nearby Hôtel Regina), it formed the basis of a priceless collection that celebrates the life, work and influence of this great artist.

This worthy collection is housed in a striking mid-17th-century villa with a cleverly painted trompe-l'oeil façade, colonnaded staircases and Italianate terraces, all set in the midst of a large olive grove on a hill in the Cimiez district of Nice (➤ 86).

The museum allows visitors an overview of Matisse's entire working life, starting with copies of Old Master paintings that he made during his apprenticeship, through an era of sober, dark-toned paintings of the 1890s (including his first personal painting, *Nature Morte aux Livres*, and *Intérieur à l'Harmonium*), his impressionist and fauvist phases *(Jeune Femme à l'Ombrelle* and *Portrait of Madame Matisse),* to the bright colours and simple shapes of his maturity, best portrayed in his decorative post-war paper cut-outs, silk-screen hangings, and works such as *Nu Bleu IV* and *Nature Morte aux Grenades*.

The museum also boasts all the bronze sculptures that Matisse ever made, and the world's largest collection of his drawings and engravings, including his illustrations for James Joyce's novel *Ulysses,* and his powerful sketches and stained-glass models for the remarkable Chapelle du Rosaire at Vence (➤ 128). There are also three temporary exhibitions held every year.

🖪 *Nice 5f (off map)* 🖂 164 avenue des Arènes-de-Cimiez ☎ 04 93 81 08 08 🕔 Apr–Sep Wed–Mon 10–6; Oct–Mar Wed–Mon 10–5. Closed hols 🖐 Moderate 🚌 15, 17, 20, 22, 25 🚊 Nice

8 Musée Océanographique, Monaco

www.oceano.mc/

Perched high on a sheer cliff, this museum of marine science with its spectacular aquarium is the finest of its kind.

Monaco's prestigious Oceanographic Museum was founded in 1910 by Prince Albert I, who was an eager oceanographer, as an institute for scientific research and to house the many marine specimens he collected on his numerous voyages.

Financed by profits from the Casino, it took 11 years and 100,000 tons of white stone from la Turbie (► 146) to build. The resulting edifice, with

its staggering 85m (279ft) sheer façade that plunges straight into the sea, is a masterpiece of monumental architecture.

The museum contains some exceptional collections of nautical instruments; marine flora and fauna, including the skeletons of a 20m (66ft) whale and a 200kg (441lb) giant turtle; models of all the magnificent ships built for the sovereign's voyages, along with the laboratory installed in his last boat, *Hirondelle II;* displays demonstrating natural sea phenomena such as waves, tides, currents and salinity; and the first submarine.

The basement houses the famed Aquarium, which exhibits thousands of rare fish with beautifully lit displays of living corals from all over the world, in a huge state-of-the-art Shark Lagoon and in 90 tanks with a direct supply of sea water. Don't miss the Pacific black-tipped sharks, the Australian leafy seadragons, the shimmering sea slugs, the luminous yellow sturgeon, the sinister black lantern-eye fish and, if you are able to spot them, the camouflaged marine chameleons.

The remainder of the building contains research laboratories specializing in the study of ocean pollution and radioactivity that were previously headed by marine explorer Jacques Cousteau.

✚ 22K ✉ avenue St-Martin, Monaco-Ville ☎ 377/93 15 36 00 🕐 Oct–Mar daily 10–6, Apr–Jun and Sep daily 9:30–7, Jul–Aug daily 9:30–7:30 💰 Expensive
🍴 Restaurant and bar (€€) 🚇 Monaco ❓ A variety of short films on marine related subjects are shown daily
ℹ 2a boulevard des Moulins ☎ 377/92 16 61 66

9 Musée Picasso, Antibes

Picasso once had a studio inside Antibes' old, seafront Château Grimaldi. Today it houses one of the world's finest collections of his works.

The Grimaldi family ruled for centuries from this beautiful 13th- to 16th-century castle, constructed following the design of an ancient Roman fort. In 1928, the city of Antibes bought the castle to house its Museum of Art, History and Archaeology. When Pablo Picasso returned to his beloved Mediterranean in 1946, after spending the war years in Paris, he found that he had nowhere suitable to work so the Mayor of Antibes lent him a room in Château Grimaldi.

After the melancholy of war, Picasso's work here took on a new dimension, reflecting the *joie de vivre* of the Mediterranean, bathed in sunny colours

and incandescent light. He combined his bold new techniques with ancient themes and mythical images, creating such masterpieces as *Le Centaur et le Navire*, *Ulysée et les Sirènes*, *Nu Couché au Lit Bleu* and his famous *Antipolis* or *La Joie de Vivre*.

Although Picasso spent only six months working here, it was one of his most prolific phases. In gratitude, he donated the complete works of this period to the castle museum, together with a lively collection of tapestries, sculptures and over 150 ceramics designed at nearby Vallauris.

Most of Picasso's works can be found on the first floor of the castle, while the ground floor contains photographs of the great master at work. Works by his contemporaries, including Léger, Ernst and Hartung, hang on the second floor in Picasso's former studio, and the sunny terrace overhanging the Mediterranean provides an amusing location for stone and bronze sculptures by Miró, Richier and Pagès, displayed among cacti, trees and flowers.

✚ 20J ✉ Château Grimaldi, place Mariéjol ☎ 04 92 90 54 20; www.antibes-juanlespins.com ⏰ At the time of writing the museum was closed for restoration work. See the website for more information ✋ Moderate 🚌 Antibes

10 Villa Ephrussi de Rothschild, St-Jean-Cap-Ferrat

Baroness Béatrice Ephrussi de Rothschild's rose-pink, belle époque palace, the Île de France, is considered the finest on the Riviera.

The flamboyant Béatrice, Baroness Ephrussi de Rothschild (1864–1934) and daughter of the Bank of France's director, was a woman of seemingly unlimited wealth who had a passion for travel and fine art. She created her dream villa here in 1912, in the glorious style of the great palaces of the Italian Renaissance, set in immaculate gardens. It took seven years to build and has sea views on all sides. She named the villa after a memorable voyage on an ocean liner, the *Île de France*, and designed the main garden in the shape of a ship's deck with a Temple of Love on the bow. She even made her 35 gardeners dress as sailors.

The interior of the villa is lavishly decorated with rare furniture (including some pieces that once belonged to Marie Antoinette), set off by rich carpets, tapestries and an eclectic collection of rare *objets d'art*, and one of the world's most beautiful collections of Vincennes and Sèvres porcelain. Despite being filled with priceless works of art, the villa has retained the atmosphere of an occupied residence.

The villa is surrounded by delightful theme gardens such as Spanish, Florentine, stone, Japanese, exotic, Provençal and rose.

➕ 21K ✉ chemin du Musée, St Jean Cap-Ferrat
☎ 04 93 01 33 09 🕐 Mid-Feb to 5 Nov daily 10–6 (7 Jul–Aug); Nov to mid-Feb Mon–Fri 2–6, Sat–Sun 10–6
✋ Expensive 🍴 Salon de thé, restaurant and terrace (€€)
🚌 Beaulieu-sur-Mer ❓ Guided tours available. Gift shop
ℹ 59 av Denis Semeria, 06230 St-Jean-Cap-Ferrat
☎ 04 93 76 08 90

Best things to do

Great places to have lunch

Café de la Place (€–€€€)

Tuck into simple bistro fare at the entrance to this picturesque hilltop village, alongside locals playing boules in the leafy square.

✉ place Général de Gaulle, St-Paul-de-Vence ☎ 04 93 32 80 03

Chez Freddy (€€)

One of the best restaurants in the cours Saleya, ideal for people-watching at the colourful daily market, and especially popular for aïoli, paellas and seafood. The giant shellfish platters are excellent value.

✉ 22 cours Saleya, Nice ☎ 04 93 85 49 99; www.chezfreddy.com
🚌 All buses

Lou Pilha Leva (€)

Niçoise fast-food, at the heart of old Nice. Try the piping hot plates of *socca, pissaladière, beignets, farcis* and other delicacies.

✉ 10 rue du Collet, Nice ☎ 04 93 13 99 08 🕒 8am–11pm (midnight in summer) 🚌 All buses

La Marine (€€)

Serving possibly the best sardines on the Corniche de l'Esterel, on a breezy terrace overhanging the Mediterranean.

✉ La figuerette, Theôule-sur-Mer ☎ 04 93 75 49 30 🕔 Closed out of season

Le Moulin de Mougins (€€€€)

It's always a treat to eat lunch in the gastronomic village of Mougins, and Le Moulin here counts among the finest restaurants of the Riviera, with a price tag to match. Ideal for special occasions.

✉ Notre-Dame de Vie, Mougins ☎ 04 93 75 78 24; www.moulin-mougins.com 🕔 Tue–Sun 12–2, 7:30–9:45. Closed Mon

L'Oasis (€€)

Dine on the beach, with stunning views from the Cap d'Antibes to the Îles de Lérins.

✉ boulevard Guillarmont, Juan-les-Pins ☎ 04 93 61 45 15

La Table du Marché (€–€€)

This cheerful bistro-cum-deli offers a tempting array of regional specialities and wines. It also serves afternoon tea.

✉ 38 rue Georges Clemenceau, St-Tropez ☎ 04 94 97 85 20; www.christophe-leroy.com 🕔 Closed Mon eve, Wed and winter

La Tarterie (€)

Delicious sweet and savoury tarts to eat in and take away. Grab a slice and eat it on the beach or alongside the ostentatious yachts.

✉ 33 rue Bivouac Napoléon, Cannes ☎ 04 93 39 67 43 🕔 Mon–Sat 8:30–6:30

Zebra Square (€€)

Rub shoulders with the beautiful people on the sun terrace at this chic restaurant where even the crockery has zebra stripes.

✉ 10 avenue Princesse-Grace, Monte-Carlo ☎ 0377 99 99 25 50

Top beaches

Cannes
The best beaches in the region for star-spotting, especially during the Cannes Film Festival when you'll see the paparazzi milling around the bay in speed boats, hoping to catch the celebrities on camera. (➤ 118–121)

Cap d'Antibes
The tiny Plage de la Garoupe here is the best alternative to your own private stretch of beach on the Cap. It is fun for children with shallow water and interesting rocks to explore. The beach is divided into sections, two of which are public. (➤ 115)

Esterel Massif
Seek out one of the many tiny sandy coves dotted along this wild and unspoilt stretch of coast to the east of Le Trayas, with its stunning backdrop of red porphyry rock.

Fréjus-Plage
Best for families – popular, sandy and gently shelving, with boat hire and plenty of water sports on offer. (➤ 173)

Îles de Lérins
Undoubtedly the best island beaches – quiet, sandy, and excellent for swimming and snorkelling. (➤ 44–45)

Juan-les-Pins
It seems only appropriate that this beautiful beach, with its fine silvery sand, put Juan-les-Pins on the map in the 1920s as the first summer resort on the Riviera. (➤ 124)

Menton
Sun-worshippers should head to Menton's beach, as this attractive Italianate town with its many semi-tropical gardens boasts the best sunshine record in France – 300 days a year. (➤ 150)

Ruhl-Plage, Nice
Out of several beaches in Nice, this one offers some of the best water sports. It was also the first beach on the coast to be on the internet, meaning visitors can 'surf' under the shade of beach umbrellas!

La Voile Rouge, St-Tropez
It was in St-Tropez that girls first dared to bathe topless in the 1960s. Several beach strips on the Baie de Pampelonne are currently fashionable. La Voile Rouge is considered the trendiest and most frivolous, and a good place for celebrity-spotting. (► 165)

Plage de la Briande, St-Tropez
In contrast to La Voile Rouge, Plage de la Briande, with its fine golden sand, is the most deserted St-Tropez beach. (► 165)

Best nightlife

Cannes Film Festival
Join Hollywood's movers and shakers and paint the town
red during the world's most celebrated movie festival
(www.festival-cannes.fr).

Casino
There's no need to break the bank to enjoy a glitzy night out at
Monte-Carlo's celebrated bastion of gambling. (➤ 36–37)

Les Caves du Roy
The place to see and be seen clubbing in St-Tropez
✉ Hôtel Byblos, avenue Paul Signac, St-Tropez ☎ 04 94 97 16 02
🕐 Easter–Oct 11pm–5am

Cinema d'Été
Relax under the stars on a balmy summer night and watch a
movie at Nice's open-air cinema.
✉ Chemin des Pêcheurs, Monte-Carlo, Monaco ☎ 377/93 25 86 80
🕐 Mid-Jun to mid-Sep

Cinemathèque
A must for cinephiles, showing original golden oldies as well as all
the latest releases.
✉ Acropolis, 3 esplanade Kennedy, Nice ☎ 04 92 04 06 66 🚌 All buses

Jimmi'z
Sip cocktails with the rich and famous at Monte-Carlo's most
prestigious nightclub.
✉ 26 avenue Princesse Grace, Monte-Carlo, Monaco ☎ 377/98 06 73 73
🕐 11:30pm–5am. Closed Mon, Tue and Nov–Easter

Opéra de Nice and Salle Garnier, Monaco
Opera buffs will enjoy these two top-notch venues on the
Côte d'Azur.
Opéra de Nice
✉ 4/6 rue St-François-de-Paule, Nice ☎ 04 92 17 40 00 🚌 All buses
Salle Garnier
✉ place du Casino, Monaco ☎ 377/98 06 28 00; www.opera.mc

La Slesta
One of the Riviera's wildest nightclubs, with open-air dancing and
all-night partying in summer.
✉ route du Bord-de-la-Mer (between Antibes and la Brague), Antibes
☎ 04 93 33 31 31 🕐 Mid-May to mid-Sep daily midnight–approx 4am.
Fri and Sat only in winter

Parks and gardens

Gardens of the Château-Musée Henri Clews, Mandelieu-la-Napoule

Mary Clews, wife of the American sculptor Henry Clews, designed the four acres of walled formal gardens which surround the eccentric fairytale castle at Mandelieu-la-Napoule. The gardens are filled with a huge variety of his sculptures from the classical to the grotesque, including some sea monsters, demons and fantastical gargoyles. (➤ 125)

Gardens of Fondation Maeght, St-Paul-de-Vence

The grounds of this dazzling art gallery consist of a series of terraces, gardens and ornamental ponds where artists and sculptors have given free rein to their inspiration. Mingling amid pine trees and exotic flowers are a Míro maze of sculptures and ceramics; a wall mosaic by Chagall; stained glass by Braque; spindly Giacometti sculptures 'walking' on the terrace; and a series of mobiles and 'moving sculptures' by Calder. (➤ 42)

Jardin Exotique, Èze

There are over 400 cacti and succulents in the exotic garden at Èze, surrounding the ruins of the castle at the summit of a rocky outcrop which plunges vertiginously into the sea. (➤ 40–41)

Jardin Exotique, Monaco

Tangled around a variety of twisting paths, footbridges and viewpoints, this dazzling collection of over six thousand cacti and succulents tumbles down the cliff edge high above Monaco-ville. Planted by Albert I, it features plants of remarkable proportions, including ten-metre high (33ft) candelabra euphorbias along the 'Candle Walk' and prickly *coussins de belle-mère* (grandmother's cushions) up to one metre in diameter. (➤ 143)

Phoenix Parc Floral, Nice
The vast 22-metre-high (72 ft) glass-and-metal 'Green Diamond' in Phoenix Park counts among the world's largest greenhouses and can be seen from the Promenade des Anglais. It contains seven different tropical climates and one of the most complete ranges of tropical plants in Europe, from tree ferns to rare orchids.

Renoir's Garden, Cagnes-sur-Mer
It is moving to imagine Renoir sitting in the warm sun here at his garden easel gazing out toward the distant sea for inspiration.
(➤ 116–117)

Villa Ephrussi de Rothschild, St-Jean-Cap-Ferrat
Following a memorable trip on the ocean liner *Île de France,* Baroness Ephrussi de Rothschild decided to create a boat-shaped garden for her rose-pink villa, overlooking the sea from all sides. Her gardeners created a total of nine ornamental gardens. (➤ 54)

Villa Kérylos, Beaulieu-sur-Mer
The ornate gardens of Villa Kérylos are superbly situated on the waterfront, with fine views of the Saint-Jean-Cap-Ferrat peninsula. (➤ 148)

Best souvenirs and gifts

Alziari

This old family shop presses its own olive oil and sells *olives de Nice* by the kilo. A wonderful Niçoise institution.

✉ 14 rue St-François-de-Paule, Nice ☎ 04 93 85 76 92; www.alziari.com.fr/
🚌 All buses ⏰ Tue–Sat 8:30–12, 2–6

Confiserie Florian

Taste before you buy the many mouth-watering products made at this jam-making factory. The crystallized fruits are a perfect gift.

✉ Pont du Loup ☎ 04 93 59 32 91; www.confiserieflorian.com ❓ Factory tours available 9–12 and 2–6:30

Fayences de Moustiers

This shop specializes in the famous white faïence pottery of the tiny Provençal village of Moustiers-Ste-Marie, with its delicate, hand-painted designs.

✉ 18 rue du Marché, Nice ☎ 04 93 13 06 03 ⏰ Mon–Sat 9:30–7

Herbier de Provence

A potpourri of locally made soaps, herbs, perfumes and bath products. *Ça sent la Provence!*

✉ 7 Descente de la Castre, St-Paul-de-Vence ☎ 04 93 32 91 51

J-L Martinetti

Arty photos, framed pictures, posters and cards of Nice and the Riviera.

✉ 17 rue de la Prefecture, Nice ☎ 04 93 85 61 30

Nougat Cochet

The regional speciality of nougat has been made here for several generations.

✉ 98 boulevard Felix Martin, St-Raphaël ☎ 04 94 95 01 67

Parfumerie Fragonard

The very finest perfumes from Provence are for sale here at Fragonard – one of the two major perfume factories in Grasse. There are also interesting guided tours (▶ 122).

✉ 20 boulevard Fragonard, Grasse ☎ 04 93 36 44 65; www.fragonard.com
🕐 Feb–Oct daily 9–6, Nov–Jan daily 9–12:30, 2–6

L'Univers du Vin

A giant wine warehouse on the road between Cagnes and Antibes, great for bargains. You can even order personalized labels.

✉ 1305 route National 7, Villeneuve-Loubet ☎ 04 93 73 73 94

Verrerie de Biot

Traditional bubble-flecked glassware from Provence's capital of glass-blowing makes an unusual souvenir or gift. Here visitors can also watch the glass-blowers demonstrating their art.

✉ chemin des Combes, Biot ☎ 04 93 65 03 00; www.verreriebiot.com

a walk around the Vieille Ville

Start at the western end of the cours Saleya.

This square is where Nice's famous outdoor flower, fruit and vegetable market is held (▶ 88), an ideal place to hear the local patois and to taste local Nissart delicacies.

Head east past the palace of the former Dukes of Savoy and the Italianate 18th-century Chapelle de la Misericorde to the yellow house at the end of the square, where Matisse once lived. Turn left into rue Gilly, then continue along rue Droite, past Palais Lascaris (▶ 94).

Rue Droite contains some of the old town's top galleries and Provence's best bread shop, Espuno (▶ 110).

Continue straight on as far as place St-François and the early morning fish market.

This is a rare inland fish market but, before the River Paillon was filled in, fishermen used to land here to sell their catch.

Continue down rue St-François. Bear right into rue du Collet, left at place Centrale along rue Centrale, then right into rue Mascoïnat until you reach place Rossetti.

Place Rossetti is dominated by the beautiful baroque Cathédrale Ste-Réparate (▶ 85), with its emerald dome of

Niçoise tiles. Enjoy a coffee in one of the cafés here or an ice-cream from Fenocchio's (➤ 107).

Leave the square along rue Ste-Réparate. At the end, turn right onto rue de la Préfecture.

The great violinist Niccolò Paganini lived and died at No 23.

A right turn opposite Paganini's house onto rue St-Gaètan takes you back to the cours Saleya.

Distance 2km (1.2 miles)
Time 1–2 hours, depending on shopping, museum and church visits
Start/end point cours Saleya ✚ *Nice 5b* 🚌 All buses
Lunch Chez Freddy (€€) (➤ 58) ✉ 22 cours Saleya ☎ 04 93 85 49 99

Stunning views

The summit of Mont Vinaigre in the Massif de l'Esterel.

The Exotic Gardens in Èze – (➤ 40–41) across to Corsica.

Frequent viewpoints along the Grande Corniche (➤ 149).

The highest point of the village of Gourdon.

The D53 road looking down over Monaco.

The Colline du Château in Nice (➤ 88).

The church tower in Port-Grimaud (➤ 175).

The outdoor lift at La Vista Palace hotel, Roquebrune, behind Monte-Carlo. Go in for dinner or a drink!

The Chemin des Collines, La Californie, in Super-Cannes, where the wealthiest of Cannes' residents live.

Les Moulins de Paillas on the St-Tropez peninsula.

Top fashion stores

Alain Manoukian
Chic, affordable women's clothing by a local Provençal designer.
Other boutiques in Monaco, Nice and St-Tropez.
✉ 107 boulevard Félix Martin, St-Raphaël ☎ 04 94 95 00 44;
www.alain-manoukian.fr 🕓 Mon–Sat 9:30–7

Ateker Rondini
Rondini's famous Roman-gladiator-style *sandales Tropeziennes*
were invented in 1927 and sales are still thriving.
✉ 16 rue Georges Clemenceau, St-Tropez ☎ 04 94 97 19 55

Blanc Bleu
Stylish, sporty fashion for both sexes.
✉ 3 rue Allard, St-Tropez ☎ 04 94 97 08 01

Bleu comme là-bas

A wacky, bright orange jewellery shop owned by a young, imaginative designer. Affordable and fun.

✉ 38 rue Grande, St-Paul-de-Vence ☎ 04 93 32 04 17

La Botterie

You'll find all the latest trends in footwear here.

✉ 14 boulevard des Moulins, Monte-Carlo, Monaco ☎ 377/93 25 80 55

Chacok

Bright colours and bold designs by a local Biot designer.

✉ route de la Mer, Biot ☎ 04 93 65 60 60; www.chacok.com

Christian Lacroix

One of several shops in the region belonging to the world-famous Provençal designer.

✉ 14 boulevard Croisette, Cannes ☎ 04 93 68 06 06; www.christian-lacroix.fr 🕙 Mon–Sat 10–7

Claire l'Insolite

Classic haute couture and glamorous swimwear for that classic 'St Trop' look.

✉ 1 rue Sibille, St-Tropez ☎ 04 94 97 10 74

Hermès

The ultimate in French chic. The steep prices in this boutique come with a lofty sea view to match.

✉ 11–15 avenue de Monte-Carlo ☎ 377/93 50 64 89; www.hermes.com 🕙 Mon–Sat 10 1, 3–7

Kid Cool

Shop here for bright, sporty clothing (age 3 months to 12 years) if you want your child to be a 'Cool Kid'.

✉ 3 rue Gambetta, St-Tropez ☎ 04 94 49 57 24

Places to take the children

Antibes Land
Amusement park with big wheel, roller coaster and even bungee jumping!

✉ route N7, Antibes ☎ 04 93 33 41 43 ⏰ Jun–Sep daily 3pm–2am

Aqualand
A fantastic waterpark with attractions for all the family, from the 'mini park jungle' paddling pool for toddlers to spectacular slides with such names as 'kamikaze', 'twister' and 'freefall' to thrill older children.

✉ Quartier le Capou, RN98, Fréjus ☎ 04 94 51 82 51; www.aqualand.fr
⏰ Jun daily 10am–6pm; Jul–Aug daily 10am–7pm

Azur Park
Exhilarating fairground rides for the whole family.

✉ Golfe de St-Tropez, Gassin ☎ 04 98 12 62 90 ⏰ Apr, Sep daily 6pm–midnight; May daily 7pm–midnight; Jun–Aug daily 8pm–1am

Grottes de St-Cézaire
A fairy-tale world of rich red caves filled with 'musical' stalactites and stalagmites.

✉ St-Cézaire-sur-Siagne ☎ 04 93 60 22 35;
www.lesgrottesdesaintcezaire.com ⏰ Mid-Nov to Feb Sun 2:30–5; Jun and Sep 10:30–12, 2–6; Jul and Aug 10:30–6:30; rest of year daily 2:30–5

Marineland
A wonderful world of sea lions, killer whales, dolphins and sharks. Children love the 'Jungle des Papillons' with exotic butterflies and huge hairy spiders.

✉ route N7, Antibes ☎ 04 93 33 49 49; www.marineland.fr ⏰ Daily 10–6 (8 on Wed and weekends). Closed mid-Jan to mid-Feb

Musée de l'Automobiliste
Older children in particular enjoy visiting the unique, radiator-

shaped Car Museum and viewing
footage of classic races.

✉ 772 chemin de Font-de-Currault (just off
autoroute A8 Nice–Cannes, exit Les Hautes
Bréguires), Mougins ☎ 04 93 69 27 80
🕓 Jun–Sep daily 10–6; Oct–May daily 10–1, 2–6

Musée National

Huge collection of dolls, dating from
18th century to Barbie.

✉ 17 avenue Princesse Grace, Monaco
☎ 377/93 30 91 26 🕓 Oct–Easter 10–12:15,
2:30–6:30; Easter–Sep 10–6:30. Closed 1 Jan,
1 May, 19 Nov, 25 Dec 🚌 4, 6

Les Terrasses de Fontvieille

The late Prince Rainier's collections of model boats and vintage
cars, and a zoo.

✉ terrasses de Fontvieille, Monaco ☎ Zoo 377/93 50 40 30; naval museum
377/92 05 28 48; classic car exhibition 377/92 05 28 56 🕓 Call for details
🚌 5, 6

Village des Tortues

One-hour tour of this remarkable 'village' (the world's only tortoise
conservation centre), with its 1,200 turtles and tortoises.

✉ 83590 Gonfaron (off *autoroute* Aix–Cannes), Gonfaron ☎ 04 94 78 26 41
🕓 Mar–Oct, daily 9–5 (6pm in summer)

Visiobulle

Discover the underwater world of 'Millionnaires' Bay' in a glass-
bottomed boat.

✉ embarcadère Courbet, Juan-les-Pins ☎ 04 93 67 02 11;
www.visiobulle.com 🕓 Apr–Jun departures at 11, 1:30, 3, 4:30; Jul, Aug 9,
10:25, 11:50, 2, 3:25, 4:50, 6:15; Sep 11, 1:30, 3, 4:30

Outdoor activities

Go fishing. Tired of lazing on the beach? Book a day trip and have a go at deep-sea fishing, then cook your catch on board (Sea Cruises Golfe-Juan ☎ 04 93 42 08 45).

Take a boat trip to Corsica from Nice's old port (SNCM ☎ 04 93 13 66 66) or rent a skippered yacht for the weekend and tour the coast in style. (Moorings, 10 quai Papacino, Nice, ☎ 04 92 80 08 99)

Visit the Îles de Lérins (Compagnie Maritime Cannoise ☎ 04 93 38 66 33) (➤ 44) to escape the glitz and glitter of the coastal resorts, to enjoy their tranquillity, and to learn more about their most celebrated resident, the 'Man in the Iron Mask'.

Rent a Harley-Davidson and cruise the streets of St-Tropez. (Espace 83 ☎ 04 94 55 80 00)

Take a helicopter from Nice airport to Monte-Carlo. (Héli Air Monaco ☎ 04 93 21 34 95)

Play golf at the Royal Mougins Golf Club, considered by many the best golf club on the Cote d'Azur (✉ 424 avenue du Roi, Mougins, 04 92 92 49 69), or at Golf Club Cannes-Mandelieu Riviera, one of Europe's largest courses (✉ route du Golf, 06210 Mandelieu-la-Napoule, 04 92 97 49 49)

Go hang-gliding – surely the ultimate way to view the Riviera. (✉ Fédération Francaise de Vol Libre, 4 rue de Suisse, Nice, ☎ 04 97 03 82 82)

Try your hand at boules, the most popular game in Southern France. There's usually a game going on at midday in such village squares as Place des Lices in St-Tropez and Place Général de Gaulle at St-Paul-de-Vence.

Horse-ride through the beautiful garrique landscapes of the Riviera. Popular areas include the Massif de l'esterel, the Massif des Maures and around Grasse.

Go deep-sea diving. The Riviera offers some of the finest diving in Europe. (✉ Centre International de Plongée, 2 ruelle des Moulins, Nice, ☎ 04 93 55 59 50)

Best places to stay

Des Arcades (€–€€)

A characterful 15th-century hotel in a splendid arcaded square, with a restaurant specializing in *spécialités paysannes provençales*.

✉ 16 place des Arcades, Biot ☎ 04 93 65 01 04

Château Èza (€€€)

Former home to Prince William of Sweden, these medieval houses have been linked together to form a luxury complex.

✉ rue de la Pise, Èze ☎ 04 93 41 12 24; www.chateaueza.com

L'Hermitage (€€€)

You need a princely sum to stay at this massive palace at the heart of Monte-Carlo, famed for its glass-domed Winter Garden foyer, its lavish pink-and-gold restaurant and its marble terrace.

✉ square Beaumarchais, Monte-Carlo ☎ 377/98 06 40 00

Hôtel Hi (€€)

Quirky new hotel with wacky furnishings, an organic 24-hour canteen, a Turkish bath and a pool on the roof.

✉ 3 avenue des Fleurs, Nice ☎ 04 97 07 26 26; www.hi-hotel.net

La Maison Blanche (€€€)

Beautiful old town house, decorated in terracotta and white, on the Place des Lices.

✉ 15 place des Lices, St-Tropez ☎ 04 94 97 52 66; www.hotellamaisonblanche.com

Le Mas de Chastelas (€€–€€€)

This traditional and picturesque 18th-century *mas* is surrounded by vineyards. Charming rooms decorated with Provençal fabrics and exceptional regional cuisine make for a memorable stay.

✉ quartier Bertaud, St-Tropez Peninsula ☎ 04 94 56 71 71; www.chastelas.com 🕐 Closed Nov–Dec

Moulin de la Camandoule (€€€)

Amid vines and olive trees, this converted 15th-century olive mill is hidden in a peaceful setting just outside the large hillside town of Fayence. The restaurant specializes in authentic Provençal cuisine.
✉ chemin de Notre-Dame-des-Cyprès, Fayence ☎ 04 94 76 00 84; www.camandoule.com

Les Roches (€€–€€€)

Humphrey Bogart, Jean Cocteau and Winston Churchill have graced the impressive guest-list of this small, luxury hotel, superbly situated on a picturesque inlet with its own private beach.
✉ 1 avenue des trois Dauphins, Aiguebelle Plage, Le Lavandou
☎ 04 94 71 05 07; www.hotellesroches.com

Villa Marie (€€€)

On the hill overlooking Pamelonne, this chic boutique hotel and spa is the place for the beautiful people.
✉ Chemin Val de Rian, Ramatuelle ☎ 04 94 97 40 22; www.villamarie.fr

Exploring

The resorts of this incredible stretch of coastline, surveyed from afar by snow-capped mountains, have virtually fused together into one giant, bustling megalopolis. The original piece of coast to which the name 'Riviera' was applied, when it began to be fashionable as a winter resort in the 19th century, was the stretch between Menton and Nice – which still evoke their belle époque grandeur. Now the term is used to include the fashionable yacht-havens of Antibes and Cannes, and a string of popular family resorts stretching as far as trend-setting St-Tropez.

Yet behind this glamorous coastline lies the authentic soul of the region: a picturesque landscape of vineyards, olive groves and fields of lavender, dotted with ancient villages. Here the pace of life is slow and villagers play boules in the shade of plane trees or laze in cafés, gazing out to the distant Côte d'Azur.

Nice

This magnificent all-year-round resort, so agreeably named 'Nice', is a vibrant city, shaped by a colourful past. It offers visitors a fascinating blend of ancient and modern, innumerable attractions, a wonderful climate, and a carefree *joie de vivre*, as it sits beside the glittering Baie des Anges (Bay of Angels), basking in the scorching Mediterranean sun.

Nice was originally founded by the Greeks in the 4th century BC, followed by the Romans, who had a settlement at Cimiez (later ruined by Saracens). Nice thrived again in the Middle Ages, first under the Counts of Provence, then under the Italian Dukes of Savoy. Unified with France only as recently as 1860, it retains a strong Italianate character, admirably combining Italian temperament and lifestyle with French finesse and *savoir-faire*.

Thanks mainly to the English, Nice was already Europe's most fashionable winter retreat by the 1860s, with exuberant belle époque hotels springing up along the fashionable palm-lined waterfront, which is aptly named Promenade des Anglais. Nearby,

the narrow alleys and vibrant markets of the Vieille Ville (Old Town) contrast boldly with the broad boulevards and designer boutiques of the modern metropolis that fans out from place Masséna, Nice's handsome main square. The entire city is cradled by the impressive vine-clad foothills of the Alpes-Maritimes.

This delightful setting has attracted many artists over the years. As a result Nice is blessed with more museums and galleries than any French town outside Paris.

✚ 21K 🛈 5 promenade des Anglais ☎ 0892 707 407; www.nicetourism.com

CATHÉDRALE ORTHODOXE RUSSE

This magnificent pink and grey Russian Orthodox church, crowned by six gleaming green onion-shaped cupolas, was built by Tsar Nicolas II in 1903 in memory of Alexander II's son Nicolas, who is buried in the grounds. The young, consumptive Tsarevich Nicolas was brought to Nice in search of good health in 1865, but to no avail. The luxurious villa in which he died was later demolished to build the cathedral and a mortuary chapel.

The interior takes the form of a Greek cross and is brimming with precious icons, frescoes and treasures. The lavish iconostasis separating the sanctuary from the nave features a striking icon of Our Lady of Kazan, painted on wood and set amid a riot of silver and precious stones. The church still conducts regular services in Russian.

www.egliseorthodoxerusse-nice.com
✚ *Nice 1d* ✉ avenue Nicolas II ☎ 04 93 96 88 02 🕑 May–Sep daily 9–12, 2:30–6; mid-Feb to Apr, Oct daily 9:15–12, 2:30–5:30; Nov to mid-Feb daily 9:30–12, 2:30–5. Closed Sun am
❓ No shorts or sleeveless shirts

CATHÉDRALE STE-RÉPARATE

Nice's beautiful baroque cathedral was built by local architect Jean-André Guibera in 1650 and dedicated to the city's patron saint, Réparate, who was martyred in Asia Minor at the tender age of 15.

The building is dominated by an 18th-century bell tower and a magnificent emerald dome of Niçoise tiles. The carefully proportioned façade, with its arcaded entrance, decorative niches and medallions, dates from 1825 and has recently been enhanced with colour.

Inside, visitors are met by a profusion of baroque marble, stucco and gilt. Note the ornate marble high altar and choir balustrade, the walnut panelling in the sacristy, acquired from Nice's Dominican convent, and the painting *Dispute du Saint-Sacrement* in the right transept, attributed to the Raphaël School.

✚ Nice 5b ✉ place Rossetti ☎ 04 93 62 34 40 🕐 Mon–Fri 8:30–11:30, 2–6 💵 Free 🚌 4, 7, 14, 17, 71, 75 ❓ No shorts or sleeveless shirts

CIMIEZ

Cimiez is a district of luxury villas and palatial residences on the low hills overlooking the city. A monument dedicated to Queen Victoria outside her favourite winter residence, the recently renovated Hôtel Regina, serves as a reminder that Cimiez was frequently visited by royalty at the turn of the century. It is still considered to be Nice's most desirable residential quarter.

As early as 140BC, the Romans built a town on the hills of Cimiez called Cemenelum which, by the end of the 2nd century AD, had 20,000 inhabitants and was the capital of the Roman Alpes Maritimae province.

The remains of a small amphitheatre (Arènes), paved streets and public baths have been excavated at the top of the Boulevard de Cimiez. A small, modern museum **(Musée d'Archéologie)** displays the finds and illustrates the city's history from the Bronze Age to medieval times.

Nearby is the Musée Matisse (➤ 48). Both museums back on to an old olive grove that is the venue for Europe's leading international jazz festival in July, attracting top celebrities from all over the world. At the eastern end of the grove is the **Monastère Franciscain de Cimiez** (Franciscan Monastery) and the church of Notre-Dame-de-l'Assomption.

The Franciscans have used the church and monastery since 1546. Inside are two masterpieces by Louis Bréa, a leading painter of the Nice School, and an impressive carved altarpiece. A museum in the monastic buildings evokes the life of Franciscan monks in Nice from the 13th to the 18th centuries. Dufy and Matisse lie buried in the adjacent cemetery overlooking Nice.

Site et Musée d'Archéologie

✝ *Nice 5f* ✉ 160 avenue des Arènes ☎ 04 93 81 59 57 ⓘ Wed–Mon 10–6. Closed Tue and some hols 🚶 Moderate 🚌 15, 17, 20, 22, 25 ❓ Guided tours by appointment

Monastère Franciscain de Cimiez

✉ place du Monastère, avenue Bellanda ☎ 04 93 81 00 04 ⓘ Mon–Sat 10–12, 3–6. Closed hols 🚶 Free 🚌 15, 17, 20, 22, 25

COLLINE DU CHÂTEAU (CASTLE HILL)

Surprisingly, there is no château here. The city's fortress was destroyed by the French in the early 18th century when Nice belonged to Savoy. Instead, you will find cool, shady gardens, which are particularly enjoyable in the summer with their fountains and absorbing views over the crowded old port (Quartier du Port ► 100–101), the gleaming, glazed tiles of the old town (Vieille Ville ► 102–103) and the voluptuous curve of the Baie des Anges.

It was on this imposing site that Nice originated as the ancient Greek acropolis of Nikaïa. Archaeologists have since discovered Roman and medieval remains, some of which have been housed in a tiny museum on the hill.

The best approach is up the steps on quai des Etats-Unis, or by lift from nearby Tour Bellanda. Descend eastwards along montée Eberlé and rue Catherine Ségurane to the elegant, arcaded place Garibaldi, which is named after the great Niçoise revolutionary Giuseppe Garibaldi (hero of Italy's unification) who lies buried in the hilltop cemetery.

🕂 *Nice 6b* ✉ Colline du Château ☎ 04 93 85 62 33 📖 Free 🍴 Café (€) 🚌 All buses ❓ Lift operates Oct–Mar daily 10–6, Apr–May and Sep daily 9–7, Jun–Aug 9–8. Lift: inexpensive

COURS SALEYA

Every morning (except Monday, which is reserved for antique dealers), this spacious, sunny square is the scene of one of France's most famous markets. The colourful stands overflow with locally grown produce, including flowers, olives, honey, tomatoes, citrus fruits and *herbes de Provence* – the tastes, fragrances and colours of Provence and Italy are a veritable feast for the senses.

Arrive at dawn and you will find the Riviera's top chefs choosing their *plats du jour* from the tempting food displays. During the day, it is fun to watch the world go by from the pavement terraces of the countless bars and restaurants that line the famous market, or to try a light snack from the market stalls.

Look for *pissaladière* (onion tart with anchovy and olives) or visit Madame Thérèse's stall for the best *socca* (traditional Niçoise chickpea pancake) in town. At night, cafés and restaurants come into their own, making this one of Nice's liveliest nightspots.

➕ *Nice 5b* ✉ cours Saleya ⏱ Fruit and vegetable market: Tue–Sun 6am–1pm. Flower market: all day except Sun pm; Flea market: Mon am 🚌 All buses

HÔTEL NÉGRESCO

Churchill, Chaplin, Piaf, Picasso, Taylor and Burton, the Beatles…
The Négresco's guest list is legendary. It was built in 1912 for
Henri Négresco, once a gypsy-violin serenader, who went
bankrupt eight years later. Nevertheless,
it remains a famous Riviera landmark, a
National Historic Monument and one of
France's most magnificent hotels.

The interior is full of surprises,
ranging from the world's largest
Aubusson carpet to gaudy, gold glittery
bathroom suites. The décor is inspired
by Versailles and the lavatories alone are
more lavishly ornamented than many
other hotel lounges.

From the outside, its pink-and-white
turreted façade looks more like a
wedding cake than a hotel. You may

have trouble finding the main entrance because it is in a small back street. The whole hotel was built backwards to protect guests from the then unfashionable sun.

www.hotel-negresco-nice.com

✚ *Nice 2a* ✉ 37 promenade des Anglais ☎ 04 93 16 64 00 🍴 Le Chantecler (€€€) (➤ 106); La Rotonde (€) (➤ 107) 🚌 3, 7, 8, 9, 10, 11, 14, 22

MAMAC

Best places to see ➤ 46—47.

MUSÉE DES BEAUX-ARTS

Once home to a Ukranian princess, this handsome residence, built in the style of 17th-century Genoese palaces, is now home to Nice's Museum of Fine Art. The collection began with a donation from Napoléon II and includes works from 17th-century Italian Old Masters right through to contemporary works. One entire gallery is given over to 18th-century Niçoise artist Carle Van Loo (1705–65) and the main staircase is adorned with the works of Jules Chéret (1836–1932), a popular belle époque lithographist, who introduced colour advertising posters to France in 1866.

The École Française is also well represented, with works by Dégas, Boudin and Sisley. Sculptures by Rodin and Carpeaux also form part of the collection, together with important impressionist and post-impressionist works by Bonnard, Vuillard and Van Dongen (including his famous *Tango of the Archangel* – an entertaining evocation of the roaring twenties on the Riviera).

The main attraction of the museum is an exceptional collection of works by the impressionist café-society artist, Raoul Dufy, moved from the old Musée Dufy on the waterfront because the salt air was affecting the paint. Of particular note are the early fauve works, the 1908 *Bâteaux à l'Estaque* (a cubist painting predating cubism), and a handful of colourful Nice scenes.

✚ *Nice 1b (off map)* ✉ 33 avenue des Baumettes ☎ 04 92 15 28 28 🕐 Tue–Sun 10–12, 2–6 💰 Moderate 🚌 3, 8, 9, 10, 12, 22, 23, 38

MUSÉE INTERNATIONAL D'ART NAÏF ANATOLY JAKOVSKY

The International Museum of Naïve Art is housed in an elegant, turn-of-the-century pink villa, the Château de Ste-Hélène, built by the perfume magnate, Coty.

It contains a remarkable 600 canvases, drawings, engravings and sculptures, donated by Anatoly Jakovsky, illustrating the history of naïve art throughout the world from the 17th century to the present day. Croatian artists are especially well represented, including Generalić, Kovačić and Petrović. Look also for French masters of the genre, including Vivin, Rimbert and Bauchant.

🚩 Nice 1a (off map) ✉ Château Ste-Hélène, avenue de Fabron ☎ 04 93 71 78 33 🕑 Wed–Mon 10–6. Closed some hols 🖐 Moderate 🚌 9, 10, 11, 12, 23, 34, 60

MUSÉE MATISSE

Best places to see ➤ 48–49.

MUSÉE NATIONAL MESSAGE BIBLIQUE MARC CHAGALL

Located in the heart of a Mediterranean garden at the foot of Cimiez hill, this striking, modern museum was especially designed by André Hermant to exhibit Marc Chagall's 'Biblical Message' – a series of 17 monumental canvases, created between 1954 and 1967, evoking the Garden of Eden, Moses and other biblical themes.

Chagall was a highly individualistic Russian-Jewish painter who drew his main themes from the Old Testament and Russian-

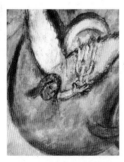

Jewish folklore. Born in Vitebsk in 1887, he spent the war years in America, before moving permanently to St-Paul-de-Vence in 1950.

He opened the museum here himself in 1973. He also created the mosaic of the prophet Elijah, cleverly reflected in the pool, and the beautiful blue stained-glass windows representing *The Creation of the World* in the concert hall. Other works were donated to the museum after Chagall's death in 1985, making this the largest and most important collection of his work.

✚ *Nice 4e* ✉ avenue Docteur Ménard ☎ 04 93 53 87 20 🕐 Jul–Sep Wed–Mon 10–6; Oct–Jun Wed–Mon 10–5. Closed 1 Jan, 1 May, 25 Dec ♿ Moderate 🍴 Garden café, Apr–Oct (€) 🚌 15 ❓ Reserve guided tours in advance (☎ 04 92 91 50 20)

PALAIS LASCARIS

In a narrow back street at the heart of the Vieille Ville, behind a façade of ornate balconies and pilasters adorned with garlands of flowers, lies the beautiful Palais Lascaris. This Genoese-style palace was originally four separate houses, bought in 1648 by the powerful Lascaris-Ventimiglia family. The city of Nice purchased the property in 1942 and has since restored this noble building.

In the entrance hall the family coat of arms is engraved on the ceiling, bearing the motto 'Not even lightning strikes us'. On the ground floor there is a reconstruction of a pharmacy dated 1738, with an unusual collection of porcelain vases. A grandiose balustraded staircase, decorated with 17th-century paintings and statues of Mars and Venus, leads to sumptuous reception rooms containing elegant chandeliers, Flemish tapestries, 17th- and 18th-century furniture, ornate woodwork and a *trompe-l'oeil* ceiling.

✚ *Nice 5b* ✉ 15 rue Droite ☎ 04 93 62 72 40 ⏰ Wed–Mon 10–6 🖐 Free 🚌 1, 2, 3, 5, 6, 8, 11, 14, 16, 17, 25, 37, 38, 60, 62, 63, 64

PALAIS MASSÉNA – MUSÉE D'ART ET D'HISTOIRE

Palais Masséna was built in the first Empire style in 1901 by Prince Victor Masséna, the great-grandson of Nice-born Marshal Masséna, Napoléon's ruthlessly ambitious military genius. The building was bequeathed to the city of Nice on the condition that it become a museum devoted to regional history.

The solemn statue of Napoléon that stands near the entrance sets the tone for the wide-ranging historical exhibits inside, which include paintings by members of the early Nice School, a library containing over 10,000 rare books and manuscripts, and a fearsome collection of 15th- and 16th-century weaponry. There are various rooms dedicated to Garibaldi, Napoléon, Marshal Masséna and the Nice plebiscite of 1860. A fascinating section is reserved for local traditions; especially enjoyable are the collections of costumes, furniture, faïence pottery (tin-glazed earthenware) and regional craftwork.

✚ *Nice 2b* ✉ 35 promenade des Anglais and 65 rue de France ☎ 04 93 88 11 37 ⏰ 10–12, 2–6 (Oct–Mar 2–5). At the time of writing the museum was closed for restoration and due to reopen in 2007 🚌 3, 7, 8, 9, 10, 11, 14, 22

a walk around Nice's gardens and promenades

Start at the Acropolis (➤ 100). Head southward, climbing up a flight of steps to MAMAC (➤ 46) and the Théâtre de Nice.

The monumental, marble-clad Museum of Modern Art (MAMAC) and the 282-million-franc Théâtre de Nice (TDN) are Nice's answer to Paris' Pompidou Centre.

Continue beyond the theatre into the gardens of the promenade du Paillon, climbing to the highest level.

These 'hanging gardens' cleverly hide a hideous concrete car park and the ugly main bus station below. Although a

pleasant place to stroll by day, this area is best avoided after dusk.

Go down the steps (to the right of the car park) and cross the road into place Général Leclerc. Continue across allée Résistance et Déportation, through espace Masséna and on to place Masséna (▶ 100).

Éspace Masséna, lined with benches and with fountains that bubble both day and night, is a popular yet peaceful place to cool off in the summer. By contrast, neighbouring place Masséna is one of Nice's busiest squares.

More gardens (Jardins Albert Ier) lead to the waterfront. Turn right on to the Promenade des Anglais (▶ 98).

The Promenade des Anglais follows the gracious curve of the Baie des Anges, past belle époque mansions and follies created by English lords and Russian aristocrats in Nice's heyday. In summer there is a small open-air theatre (Théâtre de Verdure) in the gardens.

Continue along the waterfront until you reach Hôtel Négresco (▶ 90).

Distance 2.5km (1.6 miles)
Time 1–1.5 hours
Start point Acropolis ✚ *Nice 6d* 🚌 All buses
End point Hôtel Négresco ✚ *Nice 2a* 🚌 6, 7, 9, 10, 12, airport bus
Lunch La Rotonde (€€) (▶ 107) ✉ Hôtel Négresco, 37 promenade des Anglais ☎ 04 93 16 64 00

PROMENADE DES ANGLAIS

The promenade des Anglais is one of Nice's great trademarks. As its name suggests, this palm-lined promenade, which stretches along the curvaceous Baie des Anges (Bay of Angels), was constructed at the expense of Nice's wealthy English residents in 1822, so that they could stroll along the shoreline.

Originally the promenade was a simple coastal path only 2m (6.6ft) wide. Today it is a frenetic highway of autoroute porportions and the white wedding-cake style architecture of the luxury belle époque hotels, such as the world famous Négresco (➤ 90) are now juxtaposed with ugly concrete apartment blocks.

The promenade des Anglais backs a 6km (3.7 miles) stretch

of pebble beaches, washed by a brilliant azure sea. To the north lies a cobweb of busy pedestrianized streets, brimming with restaurants, bars and chic boutiques.

✚ *Nice 2a* ✉ promenade des Anglais 🚍 3, 7, 9, 10, 11, 12, 14, 22

❓ Casino Barriére de Nice-Ruhl (▶ 111) ☎ 04 97 03 12 22; open-air theatre in Jardin Albert 1er ☎ 04 97 13 37 65

QUARTIER DU PAILLON

The once fast-flowing and often dangerously high River Paillon was canalized in the 1830s and began to vanish under the pavements. It now trickles below Nice's showcase gardens – lush Jardins Albert 1er, fountain-filled éspace Masséna, leafy Général Leclerc and the hanging gardens of the promenade du Paillon (➤ 96).

The Paillon district's main focal point is place Masséna, a stately 19th-century square featuring red-ochre buildings built across the path of the river. Many important streets fan out from the square, notably avenue Jean Médecin and rue Masséna. A balustraded terrace and steps to the south lead to the old town (Vieille Ville ➤ 102). To the north the covered course of the river provided space for several grand civic projects built during the last 25 years: a row of cultural complexes including the state-of-the-art MAMAC building (➤ 46), the **Théâtre National de Nice** and the **Acropolis** convention centre, an eyesore of concrete slabs and smoked glass.
✚ Nice 4c

Théâtre National de Nice (TNN)
✉ promenade des Arts ☎ 04 93 13 90 90 🍴 Café (€) 🚌 All buses
Acropolis
✉ 1 esplanade Kennedy ☎ 04 93 92 83 00; www.nice-acropolis.com
🚌 All buses

QUARTIER DU PORT

For centuries there was no port at Nice. Local boats simply moored in the lee of the castle rock while larger ships anchored in Villefranche Harbour. It was only in 1750 that Charles-Emmanuel III, Duke of Savoy, saw the potential trading benefits, and excavated a deep-water port at the mouth of the Lympia River.

Today Lympia port is busy with craft of all kinds, from tiny traditional fishing barques to car ferries from Corsica. It is flanked by striking red-ochre, 18th-century buildings and the neo-classical church of Notre-Dame-du-Port. It is best approached via a windy headland, aptly named quai Rauba-Capéu ('hat-thief'), past a colossal monument commemorating the 4,000 Niçoise who died during World War I. On a hill to the east, the **Musée de Terra Amata**, built on the site of an excavated fossil beach, documents prehistoric life in the region.

✚ *Nice 7b*

Musée de Terra Amata

✉ 25 boulevard Carnot ☎ 04 93 55 59 93 🕑 Tue–Sun 10–6. Closed some hols 🖐 Moderate 🚌 1, 2, 7, 9, 10, 14, 20, 30, 32

VIEILLE VILLE

The best way to discover Nice is to get lost in the tangle of dark, narrow streets of the Vieille Ville (Old Town), festooned with flowers and laundry and brimming with cafés, hidden squares and bustling markets. Dismissed as a dangerous slum in the 1970s, this is now the trendiest and most scenic part of Nice, with its stylish Italianate buildings painted in sunny terracotta reds with cool green shutters.

In the back streets, designer boutiques, galleries and intimate Nissart restaurants rub shoulders with no-nonsense workers' cafés and run-of-the-mill stores catering for the daily needs of the locals. The rue du Marché, rue de la Boucherie, rue du Collet and rue Pairolière have the atmosphere of a covered market, lined with photogenic food stalls. For early risers, a visit to the pungent fish market on place St-François is an interesting experience.

The old town's heart beats loudest at the cours Saleya (➤ 88). Lively both day and night, with its enticing daily market, al fresco restaurants, cafés and clubs, it also contains some striking architecture, including the Église de l'Annonciation, one of the

oldest churches in Nice, and the Chapelle de la Miséricorde, with its Piedmontese baroque façade and flamboyant rococo interior.

Nearby are several quirky art galleries including the **Galerie de la Marine** and the vaulted **Galerie des Ponchettes**, which was formerley used as an arsenal for the Sardinian navy then as a fish market until Matisse persuaded the local authorities to renovate it in 1950. Both stage temporary exhibitions.

✚ *Nice 5b*

Galerie de la Marine

✉ 59 quai des Etats-Unis ☎ 04 93 91 92 90
🕐 Tue–Sun 10–6. Closed hols 🖐 Free 🚌 1, 2, 14

Galerie des Ponchettes

✉ 77 quai des Etats-Unis ☎ 04 93 62 31 24
🕐 Tue–Sun 10–6. Closed hols 🖐 Free 🚌 All buses

HOTELS

Acanthe (€)

This friendly hotel just a stone's throw from Place Masséna is a long-time favourite of budget travellers in Nice. Comfortable and clean. Fifty per cent discount on Plage Galion.

✉ 2 rue Chauvain ☎ 04 93 62 22 44; www.hotel-acanthe.com 🚌 All buses

Le Beau Rivage (€€€)

Matisse spent two years here and Chekhov, during his stay, wrote *The Seagull* in this elegant hotel, newly refurbished and strategically placed on the waterfront near the opera and old town.

✉ 24 rue St-François-de-Paule ☎ 04 92 47 82 82; www.nicebeaurivage.com
🚌 3, 6, 9, 10, 12, 14

Hôtel Hi (€€)

See pages 78–79.

Négresco (€€€)

World-famous hotel built in the classic wedding-cake style (➤ 90).

✉ 37 promenade des Anglais ☎ 04 93 16 64 00;
www.hotel-negresco-nice.com 🚌 3, 7, 8, 9, 10, 11, 14, 22

Palais Maeterlinck (€€€)

A palatial, modern coastal hotel with terraced gardens, a first-class restaurant and a private beach accessed by cable-car.

✉ 30 boulevard Maurice Maeterlinck ☎ 04 92 00 72 00;
www.palais-maeterlinck.com 🚌 14

Palais de la Méditerranée (€€€)

After 25 years of closure, this luxury seafront hotel has undergone a major facelift. Now behind its magnificent art deco façade are 188 lavish rooms and suites, a pool and a spa.

✉ Promenade des Anglais ☎ 04 92 14 77 00;
www.lepalaisdelamediterranee. com

La Pérouse (€€€)

On the edge of old Nice, this modern hotel with rustic décor enjoys a view along the Baie des Anges.

✉ 11 quai Rauba-Capéu ☎ 04 93 62 34 63; www.hotel-la-perouse.com
🚌 38

Le Petit Palais (€€)

This charming belle époque hotel was once the home of the actor/writer Sacha Guitry. Located in Cimiez it has small, well-appointed rooms and wonderful views of the roofs of the town and the sea beyond.

✉ 17 avenue Emile Biéckert ☎ 04 93 62 19 11; www.petitpalaisnice.com

Solara (€)

Excellent value in Nice's chic pedestrian zone. Reserve early.

✉ 7 rue de France ☎ 04 93 88 09 96

Windsor (€€)

This eccentric hotel, just five minutes' walk from the sea, features an English-style pub, a Turkish bath and Thai-style lounges and an exotic garden with pool.

✉ 11 rue Dalpozzo ☎ 04 93 88 59 35; www.hotelwindsornice.com
🚌 3, 9, 10, 14

RESTAURANTS

L'Acchiardo (€)

One of the few authentic café bar/restaurants remaining in old Nice, serving simple, nourishing dishes at reasonable prices, and probably the best *soupe de poissons* in Nice.

✉ 38 rue Droite ☎ 04 93 85 51 16 🕓 Closed Sat eve, Sun and Mon
🚌 All buses

Aphrodite (€€)

The imaginative culinary creations of young chef David Faure are a seductive blend of classic French and Nissart cuisine.

✉ 10 bd Dubonchage ☎ 04 93 85 63 53; www.restaurant-aphrodite.com
🕓 Closed Sun and Mon 🚌 37, 38

Auberge de Théo (€)

This friendly trattoria-style restaurant in Cimiez serves delicious pizzas and copious salads.

✉ 52 av Cap de Croix ☎ 04 93 81 26 19; www.auberge-de-theo.com
🕐 Closed Mon and Sun 🚌 15, 25

Le Chantecler (€€€)

Nice's leading restaurant – a bastion of French gastronomy and a truly memorable dining experience.

✉ Hôtel Négresco, 37 promenade des Anglais ☎ 04 93 16 64 00; www.hotel-negresco.com 🕐 Daily 12:30–2:30, 7:30–10:30 🚌 3, 7, 8, 9, 10, 11, 14, 22

Chez Freddy (€€)

See pages 58–59.

Le Comptoir (€€)

Classical cuisine in a chic turn-of-the-century brasserie, decorated with art-deco panelling, mirrors and lights, and currently very 'in'.

✉ 20 rue St-François-de-Paule ☎ 04 93 92 08 80 🕐 Closed Sat and Sun lunch 🚌 All buses

Don Camillo (€€€)

This small undistinguished-looking restaurant is a bastion of Italo-Nissart cuisine. Don't miss the homemade ravioli filled with Swiss chard and the best tiramisu in the region.

✉ 5 rue des Ponchettes ☎ 04 93 85 67 95 🕐 Closed Sun and Mon lunch 🚌 All buses

L'Estocaficada (€€)

The regional dishes in this atmospheric bistro are made from ingredients straight from the nearby market.

✉ 2 rue de l'Hôtel de Ville ☎ 04 93 80 21 64 🕐 Closed Sun and Mon, except for private parties 🚌 All buses

L'Estrilha (€€)

A popular restaurant in the old town and a must for ravioli fans, with a wide choice of delicous sauces.

✉ 13 rue de l'Abbaye, Vieille Ville ☎ 04 93 62 62 00 🚌 All buses

Fenocchio (€)

The best ice cream on the Côte d'Azur.

✉ 2 place Rossetti ☎ 04 93 80 72 52 🕐 9am–midnight 🚌 All buses

Flo (€€)

A brasserie-style restaurant in a converted art-deco theatre with the kitchen on the stage! Special late-night menu up to midnight.

✉ 4 rue Sacha Guitry ☎ 04 93 13 38 38; www.flonice.com 🚌 1, 2, 4, 5, 9, 10, 14, 22, 23, 24

Le Grand Café du Turin (€€)

This cosy café serves Nice's best shellfish. Order oysters by the dozen or *coquillages* by the kilo.

✉ 5 place Garibaldi ☎ 04 93 62 29 52 🚌 3, 7, 9, 10, 14

Lou Pilha Leva (€)

See pages 58–59.

La Mérenda (€€)

An irresistable menu of 'Nissart' specialities lovingly prepared by one of France's outstanding chefs.

✉ 4 rue de la Terrace 🕐 Closed weekends and hols 🚌 All buses
❓ Credit cards not accepted

La Petite Maison (€€€)

This restaurant offers local market-fresh dishes near the Opéra. The *hors d'oeuvres Niçoise* is a meal in itself. It is advisable to reserve a table well in advance.

✉ 11 rue St-François-de-Paule ☎ 04 93 92 59 59 🕐 Closed Sun
🚌 All buses

La Rotonde (€€)

La Rotonde is the Riviera's most original brasserie. A circular restaurant with bright merry-go-round décor, complete with flashing lights, automats and painted wooden horses.

✉ Hôtel Négresco, 37 promenade des Anglais ☎ 04 93 16 64 00;
www.hotel-negresco-nice.com 🕐 7am–11:30pm 🚌 3, 7, 8, 9, 10, 11, 14, 22

La Zucca Magica (€)

A simple vegetarian restaurant beside the city's old port. Run by an award-winning chef from Rome, it offers excellent value.

✉ 4 bis quai Papacino ☎ 04 93 56 25 27 🕐 Closed Sun and Mon 🚌 1, 2, 7

SHOPPING

ART AND ANTIQUES

Atelier Galerie Dury

Contemporary paintings, sculptures and reliefs with a nautical theme by award-winning artist Christian Dury.

✉ 31 rue Droite, Vieille Ville ☎ 04 93 62 50 57 🚌 All buses

Atelier Galerie Sylvie T

Paintings, sketches and postcards of architecture typical to Nice.

✉ 14 rue Droite ☎ 04 93 62 59 15; www.sylvie-t.com

Galerie Boutique Ferrero

Exponents of the Second Nice School (Klien, Rayasse, César, Arman, Ben and Tinguely) – very modern and very expensive.

✉ 2 rue du Congrès ☎ 04 93 88 34 44 🕐 Mon–Sat 10–12:30, 2:30–7

J-L Martinetti

See pages 66–67.

Tourette

Antique clocks, watches and musical boxes have been Monsieur Tourette's speciality here for over 30 years.

✉ 17 rue Lépante ☎ 04 93 92 92 88

FASHION

Agnès B

A chic boutique selling stylish *prêt-à-porter* classics.

✉ 17 rue des Ponchettes ☎ 04 93 62 32 39 🕐 Mon–Sat 10–7

Façonnable
This famous menswear store began in a small boutique in Nice.
✉ 7, 9 & 10 rue Paradis ☎ 04 93 87 88 80; www.faconnable.com

FOOD AND DRINK
Alziari
See pages 66–67.

Caprioglio
Wine store in old Nice, to suit all purses.
✉ 16 rue de la Préfecture ☎ 04 93 85 71 36 🚌 All buses

Chocolats Puyricard
Puyricard's chocolates are considered the finest in France.
✉ 40 rue Pastorelli ☎ 04 93 85 34 30

Domaine Massa
Hidden in the steep, sun-soaked hills behind Nice, this old farm
cultivates two distinctly Niçoise products – carnations and Bellet
wine. Phone in advance for a tasting.
✉ 596 chemin de Crémat, 06200 Nice ☎ 04 93 37 80 02 🚌 62

Espuno
One of France's premier bakeries. Try the regional *fougasse* (a
herb flat bread).
✉ 35 rue Droite ☎ 04 93 80 50 67 🚌 All buses

Pâtisserie Cappa
Mouth-watering cakes and pastries to take away or eat in the tiny
tea room. Try the irresistible *tourte de blettes* – a local apple tart.
✉ 7–9 place Garibaldi ☎ 04 93 62 30 83 🚌 3, 5, 6, 7, 9, 10, 14

Maison Auer
Nice's last traditional maker of crystallised fruits. Apricots, figs,
clementines and pears that melt in your mouth.
✉ 7 rue St-François-de-Paule ☎ 04 93 85 77 98; www.maison-auer.com
🕐 Tue–Sat 9–1:30, 2:30–6 🚌 All buses

GIFTS AND SOUVENIRS
L'Atelier des Jouets
A magical shop full of sturdy, educational toys and games in wood, metal and cloth.

✉ 1 place de l'Ancien Sénat ☎ 04 93 13 09 60 ⏰ Mon–Sun 10:30–7. Closed Wed am

Fayences de Moustiers
See pages 66–67.

Halogene
You will find everything imaginable for a trendy home in this chic, modern interior design shop, including unusual furniture, lighting and gift ideas.

✉ 21/23 rue de la Buffa ☎ 04 93 88 96 26 ⏰ Tues–Sar 10–12:30, 2:30–7

Go Sport
The department store for sports fanatics with sections dedicated to every sport imaginable.

✉ 13 place Masséna ☎ 04 93 92 86 10; www.go-sport.com ⏰ Mon–Sat 10–7:30

Nocy-Bé
Ecological, educational gifts from around the world.

✉ 4 and 6 rue Jules Gilly ☎ 04 93 85 52 25 ⏰ Daily 4pm–12:30am

Parfums Poilpot
A tiny perfumery offering a wide choice of scents from Grasse. Specialties here include 'Soleil de Nice' and 'Bouquet de Nice'.

✉ 10 rue St-Gaëtan ☎ 04 93 85 60 77 🚌 All buses ⏰ Mon–Sat 10–12:30, 3–6 (and all day in the summer)

Quand le Chat n'est pa là
If you are unable to visit Monaco's Grand Prix, you will find perfect replicas of the cars among the many treasures of this toy shop.

✉ Nice Airport, Terminals 1 and 2

Transparence

As the name suggests, everything in this shop is see-through – paperweights, lampstands, trays, keyrings and more.

✉ 2 rue Jules Gilly ☎ 04 93 13 91 67 ⏰ Mon–Sat 10:30–6

ENTERTAINMENT

NIGHTLIFE AND CINEMAS

Le Before

One of the most beautiful nightclubs on the Riviera.

✉ 18 rue du Congrès ☎ 04 93 87 85 59 ⏰ 6pm–2:30am

Casino Barrière de Nice-Ruhl

Nice's glitzy, glamorous casino offers spectacular dinner cabarets as well as private gaming rooms.

✉ promenade des Anglais ☎ 04 97 03 12 22 ⏰ 10am–4am (5am Fri–Sat)

Cinémathèque

See pages 62–63.

Cinema d'Été, Nice

See pages 62–63.

Le Grand Escurial

Nice's largest indoor nightclub draws crowds of all ages for its guest DJs and popular sounds, ranging from house to R&B. Free breakfast is served at 4am.

✉ 29 rue Alphonse Karr ☎ 04 93 82 37 66 ⏰ Midnight–4.

Le Guest

A popular Niçoise nightspot in the old port, enhanced with trendy modernist décor. Dance floor.

✉ 5 quai des deux Emmanuels ☎ 04 93 56 83 83 ⏰ Open daily 11:30pm–5am 🚌 2, 9, 10

La Suite

A trendy after-dinner venue with theatrical baroque décor. Cocktail evenings and fancy-dress theme nights are popular with tourists.

✉ 2 rue Bréa ☎ 04 93 92 92 91 🕐 Mon–Sat 10:30–2:30am 🚌 All buses

THEATRE AND CLASSICAL MUSIC
L'Acropolis
This vast, modern congress, arts and tourism centre is popular for theatre, films and concerts.

✉ 1 esplanade Kennedy ☎ 04 93 92 83 00; www.nice-acropolis.com
🚌 All buses

Opéra de Nice
Home of the Nice Opera, the Philharmonic Orchestra and Ballet Corps, this rococo extravaganza in red and gold is modelled on the Naples Opera House.

✉ 4/6 rue St-François-de-Paule ☎ 04 92 17 40 00 🚌 All buses

Théâtre National de Nice (TNN)
A modern theatre containing two auditoriums, and presenting world-class shows.

✉ promenade des Arts ☎ 04 93 13 90 90 🚌 All buses

SPORTS
Centre International de Plongée
The Riviera offers some of the finest scuba diving in Europe.

✉ 2 ruelle des Moulins, Nice 🕐 04 93 55 59 50; www.cip-nice.com

Lawn Tennis Club, Nice
Venue of the Nice Open and former club of French tennis star Yannick Noah.

✉ 5 avenue Suzanne Lenglen ☎ 04 92 15 58 00

Moorings
Why not rent a skippered yacht for the weekend and visit the island of Corsica?

✉ 10 quai Papacino ☎ 04 92 00 08 99

Cannes Coast

The Cannes coast boasts some of the finest golden sandy beaches of the Riviera and some of its most celebrated resorts, including Cagnes with its fashionable race course; the major yachting haven of Antibes; and glitzy Cannes – famed for its International Film Festival.

Cannes

This region has been blessed with more than its fair share of beautiful scenery and treasures. Gastronomy reigns supreme at Mougins and Villeneuve-Loubet, and celebrated art galleries abound, including Musée Renoir at Cagnes, Musée Picasso at Antibes and Fondation Maeght in St-Paul-de-Vence. After all, this is the cradle of impressionism, and the surrounding countryside is painted with all the vivid colours of Picasso, Renoir and Matisse.

Picture-postcard villages such as Biot, Fayence and Tourrettes-sur-Loup, rich in local arts and architecture, bear witness to an eventful past. Ornamental fountains splash in the sleepy squares while villagers play boules under shady plane trees. At Grasse, the perfume capital of the world, the air is filled with all the scents of Provence, while the surrounding countryside is striped with neat rows of lavender, stretching like mauve corduroy across the landscape towards olive groves, scented fig trees and fragrant garrique scrubland.

ANTIBES

Antibes was founded in the 5th century BC as a Greek trading post called Antipolis ('the city opposite'), presumably because of its location opposite Nice, or Nikaïa. The two cities later became true opposites, with Antibes as the frontier town of France

while Nice was controlled by the Dukes of Savoy until the 18th century. Hence Vauban's mighty 17th-century Fort Carré on the eastern edge of the town, where Napoléon was once held prisoner, and the massive ancient ramparts, which today protect the old town of Antibes from flooding.

Tucked just behind the ramparts is Vieux Antibes (Old Antibes), a honey-coloured quarter of winding, cobbled lanes, splashed with flowers and overflowing with shops, restaurants and bars. Be sure to visit the bustling morning market in the cours Masséna, and the craft market which takes place Friday and Sunday afternoons (also Tuesday and Thursday in summer).

Alongside the market stands a 12th- to 16th-century seafront château, the former seat of the Grimaldi family, that today houses one of the world's finest

Picasso collections (➤ 52). Beside the castle, the bold red and yellow Église de l'Immaculée Conception represents a hotchpodge of periods and styles. Its 11th-century belfry was formerly the town's main watchtower.

On the waterfront, the Port Vauban Yacht Harbour boasts some of the Riviera's most luxurious yachts. Nearby, the Cap d'Antibes promontory was the first coastal resort to welcome rich tourists in the mid-19th century. Its beach is still considered by many the best place to enjoy the sun.

🕂 20J

🛈 11 place du Général de Gaulle ☎ 04 97 23 11 11

BIOT

The pretty hilltop village of Biot is set in a typical Provençal landscape of cypresses, olives and pines. The village encompasses a mass of steep, cobbled lanes and quaint sand-coloured houses with orange-tiled roofs.

For centuries, Biot has been a prosperous pottery centre. It is also known for its gold and silverwork, ceramics, olive wood carvings and thriving glassworks. The crafters' wares can be admired in the **Musée d'Histoire Locale et de Céramique Biotoise** while, at the Verrerie de Biot (▶ 66), visitors can watch glass-blowers demonstrating their unique *verre bullé* (bubble glass).

Twenty minutes' stroll from the old village is the **Musée Fernand Léger,** with a brilliantly coloured mosaic façade and huge stained-glass windows. The cubist painter Léger bought a villa here in 1955, intending to make Biot his home, but sadly died 15 days later. His widow founded the museum in 1959 which contains nearly 400 of his works.

www.biot.fr

✚ 20J

ℹ️ rue St Sébastien 46 ☎ 04 93 65 78 00

Musée d'Histoire Locale et de Céramique Biotoise

✉ place de la Chapelle ☎ 04 93 65 54 54 🕐 Wed–Sun 10–6

✋ Inexpensive

Musée Fernand Léger

✉ Chemin du Val de Pome ☎ 04 92 91 50 30 🕐 Oct–Jun Wed–Mon 10–12:30, 2 –5:30; Jul–Sep Wed–Mon 10:30–6. Closed Tues and some hols

✋ Inexpensive

CAGNES-SUR-MER

Cagnes is divided into three: the main beach area and old fishing quarter of Cros-de-Cagnes; Cagnes-Ville, a busy commercial centre with a racecourse right beside the sea; and Haut-de-Cagnes. This inviting hilltop village, with its brightly coloured houses, is encircled by medieval ramparts and crowned by a 14th-century castle, built

as a pirate lookout by Admiral Rainier Grimaldi. The castle contains the **Château-Musée,** which houses several exhibitions, including the Olive Tree Museum and the Museum of Modern Mediterranean Art, with works by Chagall, Matisse and Renoir.

Pierre-Auguste Renoir spent the last 12 years of his life just outside Cagnes at Domaine des Collettes. His villa, set amid 1,000-year-old olive trees, is now the **Musée Renoir.** Despite the rheumatoid arthritis that had forced him to leave Paris for a slightly warmer climate, he still spent every day sitting at his easel with his paintbrush strapped to his fingers. His palette, wheelchair and other mementoes have been preserved, together with several examples of his work; the museum also contains works by other artists such as Bonnard and Dufy.

www.cagnes-tourisme.com

✚ 20K

📋 G boulevard Maréchal Juin ☎ 04 93 20 61 G4

Château-Musée de Cagnes

✉ place Grimaldi, Haut-de-Cagnes ☎ 04 92 02 47 30 🕐 Wed–Mon 10–12, 2–5 (until 6pm from May–Sep) ✋ Inexpensive

Musée Renoir

✉ 19 chemin des Collettes ☎ 04 93 20 61 07 🕐 May–Sep Wed–Mon 10–12, 2–6; Oct–Apr 10–12, 2–5. Closed Nov ✋ Inexpensive

CANNES

Think Cannes, think movies and film stars, expensive boutiques, palatial hotels and paparazzi. After all, it is one of the world's most chic resorts – the 'Queen of the coast', 'Pearl of the Riviera' – twinned with Beverly Hills and, within France, second only to Paris for shopping and major international cultural and business events, including the world-famous Cannes International Film Festival.

With so much glitz and glamour, it is easy to forget Cannes' humble origins as a simple fishing village, named after the canes and reeds of the surrounding marshes, since transformed into luxury yacht havens. Cannes was first put on the map in 1834 by retired British Chancellor Lord Brougham, who was forced to stop in Cannes en route to Nice. Enchanted by its warm climate and quaint setting, he abandoned his former plans, built a villa here and stayed for 34 winters, singing the praises of Cannes to his most distinguished compatriots! Shortly afterwards hundreds of gentry and royals followed his example. Grand hotels began to spring up along the waterfront and by the end of the century Cannes had become the 'aristocracy's winter lounge'.

In the 1920s, Cannes adopted a rhyme: 'Menton's dowdy, Monte's brass, Nice is rowdy, Cannes is class!'. However, it was not until the 1930s that Cannes became a summer resort, made fashionable by visiting Americans, including Harpo Marx and Scott and Zelda Fitzgerald, who used to frequent the gaming tables of Casino Croisette. By the 1950s mass summer tourism had taken off and it has been the life-blood of Cannes ever since.

Admittedly Cannes lacks the great museums, galleries and monuments of other large resorts or towns, but there is always plenty to do, with its casinos, fairs, beaches, boat trips to the Îles de Lérins (➤ 44), and its luxury boutiques, which flank the waterfront and the main shopping street, rue d'Antibes.

The town is divided into two parts: modern Cannes to the east and the old Roman hilltop town of *Canois Castrum* (now known as le Suquet) on a small hill to the west. This district was Cannes' original fishing village and, appropriately, *Le Suquet* is also the Provençal name for a kind of fish soup! Unlike much of the town, it has managed to preserve the air of warmth and intimacy of bygone days. Its lively lanes of fishermen's cottages have been transformed into cosy restaurants, and the district is crowned by an imposing castle and watchtower affording sweeping coastal views.

Cannes' castle was constructed by the Lérins monks in the 11th and 12th centuries, together with a small chapel, and houses the **Musée de la Castre** containing archaeological and ethnographical collections from all over the world. The austere church in the centre of the old town, Notre-Dame d'Espérance, was built in 1648 when the chapel became too small.

At the foot of the hill, in the Vieux Port (Old Port), bobbing fishing craft are juxtaposed with millionaires' yachts. Nearby, the daily covered market – Marché Forville – presents mouth-watering displays of regional produce while the allée de la Liberté, shaded by plane trees, provides the backdrop both for boules and a vibrant morning flower market.

To the east, modern Cannes is built round la Croisette, Europe's most elegant seaside promenade, lined with palms, grand belle époque hotels and the sparkling bay with its golden beaches (of imported sand to cover the natural pebbles!). The main hotels in Cannes have their own beaches, each with bars, restaurants and immaculate rows of coloured parasols and plush lounge chairs. La Croisette has been a focus for the paparazzi since Brigitte Bardot graced Cannes' beaches in 1953. Today the most likely place to spot celebrities is at the Hôtel Carlton or Hôtel Martinez (➤ 130), especially during the International Film Festival.

This famous film festival is centred around the ugly, ultra modern **Palais des Festivals et des Congrès** on the waterfront near the flower market. Even if you don't meet any movie stars face to face, you can see their handprints immortalized in the paving stones of the allée des Stars – including Polanski, Bronson, Depardieu, even Mickey Mouse.

✚ 19H

🛈 Esptonade Georges Pompidou ☎ 04 92 99 84 22 ❓ Marché Forville: daily morning market (closed Mon in summer, Mon–Tue in winter)

Musée de la Castre

✉ Château de la Castre, le Suquet ☎ 04 93 38 55 26 🕐 Oct–Mar Tue–Sun 10–1, 2–5; Apr–Jun Tue–Sun 10–1, 2–6; Jul–Aug 10–7; Sep 10–1, 2–6; Jun–Aug open to 9 on Wed. Closed Mon and hols ♿ Inexpensive

Palais des Festivals et des Congrès

✉ 1 la Croisette ☎ 04 93 39 01 01; www.palaisdesfestivals.com 🚌 8 ❓ International Film Festival in May

FAYENCE

This large hillside town is a popular centre for local arts. The steep, narrow streets of the old town brim with the studios of local artists, weavers, potters, coppersmiths, stone and wood carvers.

Fayence is ringed by a number of picturesque villages, also well known for their arts and crafts.

www.paysdefayence.com

✚ 16J ❓ Pays de Fayence music festival in August
🛈 place Léon Roux ☎ 04 94 76 20 08

FONDATION MAEGHT

Best places to see ➤ 42–43.

GRASSE

The ancient town of Grasse is a feast for the senses. Visit on a still day, and you will find sweet floral fragrances lingering in the air, as Grasse has been the centre of the world's perfume industry for the past 400 years. Come on a clear, sunny day, and the memorable views towards the coast will explain why it has earned the nickname 'Balcony of the Côte d'Azur'.

The mild climate, rich soil and cradle of mountains sheltering the town from the harsh north winds make Grasse ideal for flower production almost all year round. Acre upon acre of the surrounding terraced countryside is used to cultivate aromatic herbs and flowers: mimosa in spring, roses and jasmine in summer; in the autumn, rows of purple lavender stripe the landscape above the town. Until recently around 85 per cent of the world's flower essence was created here, and even now this sleepy, fragrance-filled town is France's leading centre for the cut-flower market.

Somewhat surprisingly for such a sweet-scented place, Grasse started out in the Middle Ages as a tannery town, filled with all the nauseating smells of the leather industry. By the 16th century, local Italian glove-makers began to use local flowers to perfume their gloves (a fashion made popular by Catherine de Medici), and Grasse rapidly became an important perfume centre.

You can learn more about the history of Grasse and the alchemy of the perfume industry at the fascinating **Musée International de la Parfumerie,** which also has an ornate collection of labels, boxes, small chests and scent bottles (including art-nouveau glass by Lalique). The tour ends in the museum's fragrant rooftop greenhouse.

There are two main perfume factories in Grasse: the largest, **Maison Fragonard,** is named after a beloved 18th-century local artist, Jean-Honoré Fragonard (whose works can be viewed at the Musée Fragonard), while at Galimard's **Studio des Fragrances,** you can even create your own personal fragrance.

Apart from the perfumeries, Grasse has an attractive old quarter to explore. The place aux Aires, a lovely fountain-splashed square, is the scene of a vibrant morning flower market. Nearby, the austere limestone cathedral of Notre-Dame-de-Puy contains Fragonard's *Lavement des Pieds* (Washing of the Feet) and two treasured Rubens paintings, *Crucifixion* and *Courronnement*

d'Épines (Crown of Thorns). At the edge of the old town, the **Musée Provençal du Costume et du Bijou** and the **Musée d'Art et d'Histoire de Provence** provide rare insights into local culture, traditions and treasures.

www.grasse-riviera.com

✚ 18K ℹ Palais des Congrès, 22 cours Honoré Cresp ☎ 04 93 36 66 66

Musée International de la Parfumerie

✉ 8 place du Cours ☎ 04 97 05 58 00
🕐 Jun–Sep Wed–Mon 10–6; Oct–May 10–12:30, 2–5.30. Closed Nov and hols
💷 Moderate

Maison Fragonard

✉ 20 boulevard Fragonard ☎ 04 93 36 44 65; www.fragonard.com 🕐 Feb–Oct daily 9–6:45; Nov–Jan daily 9–12:30, 2–6 💷 Free

Studio des Fragrances Galimard

✉ 5 route de Pégomas ☎ 04 93 09 20 00; www.galimard.com 🕐 Daily by appointment 💷 Free but charge to create your own perfume

Musée Provençal du Costume et du Bijou

✉ Hôtel de Clapiers Cabris, 2 rue Jean Ossola ☎ 04 93 36 44 65 🕐 Mon–Sat 10–1, 2–6. Closed Nov–Jan 💷 Free

Musée d'Art et d'Histoire de Provence

✉ 2 rue Mirabeau ☎ 04 93 36 80 20 🕐 Jun–Sep daily 10–12:30, 1:30–6:30; Oct–May Wed–Mon 10–12:30, 2–5:30. Closed Nov 💷 Inexpensive

ÎLES DE LÉRINS

Best places to see ➤ 44–45.

JUAN-LES-PINS

Juan-les-Pins became the first summer resort on the Riviera in the 1920s, thanks to Nice restaurateur Edouard Baudoin, who saw a film about Miami Beach and decided to re-create it on the

Côte d'Azur. In 1924, he bought a stretch of land and opened a restaurant and a small casino. By 1930 Juan-les-Pins had become not only the most popular resort, but also the most scandal-ridden, as the first beach in France where young women dared to bathe in one-piece swimsuits without skirts.

Today it remains a popular resort renowned for its lively nightlife. Yet it maintains a certain sophistication, thanks to its chic shops, pine-fringed beach and famous jazz festival.

www.antibes-juanlespins.com

✚ 20H

🛈 51 boulevard Charles Guillaumont ☎ 04 97 23 11 10

❓ International Jazz Festival for two weeks in July. Tickets from Office de Tourisme

MANDELIEU-LA NAPOULE

The underrated resorts of Mandelieu-la Napoule lie in the shadow of their glamorous neighbour, Cannes. Inland, Mandelieu is known for golf, boasting one of the largest golf courses in Europe.

The sister town of la Napoule has three sandy beaches and a large marina, but its main attraction is a seaside fairy-tale castle **(Château-Musée Henri Clews)**, built in 1919 by Henry Clews, an American millionaire and sculptor, as a refuge from the modern world. This pseudo-medieval fantasy castle and gardens is decked out with Clews' eccentric sculptures and artwork.

www.ot-mandelieu.fr

✚ 18H

🛈 Mandelieu: avenue de Cannes ☎ 04 92 97 99 27; la Napoule: avenue Henri-Clews ☎ 04 93 49 95 31

Château-Musée Henri Clews

⏱ 7 Feb–7 Nov daily 10–6; 8 Nov–10 Feb Mon–Fri 2–5, Sat–Sun 10–5. Guided tours throughout the day ☎ 04 93 49 95 05; www.chateau-lanapoule.com 💶 Moderate

MOUGINS

Outwardly Mougins seems a typical Provençal hill village but, once inside its medieval ramparts, you will find one of the Riviera's smartest villages, whose past residents have included Jacques Brel, Yves Saint Laurent, Catherine Deneuve and Picasso – who spent the last 12 years of his life here. Numerous celluloid portraits of him can be seen in the **Musée de la Photographie.**

Mougin's main attraction, though, is the sheer number of renowned restaurants. People come from miles around to dine at La Terrasse à Mougins, Le Candille or, for a real treat, Le Moulin de Mougins (➤ 58), which is considered to be one of the world's most prestigious gourmet temples.

www.mougins-coteazur.org

🕂 19J

🛈 15 avenue Jean Charles Mallet

☎ 04 93 75 87 67

Musée de la Photographie

✉ porte Sarrazine, Mougins

☎ 04 93 75 85 67 🕓 Dec–Oct Mon–Fri 10–6, Sat–Sun and hols 11–6. Closed Nov 👋 Inexpensive

MUSÉE PICASSO

Best places to see ➤ 52–53.

ST-PAUL-DE-VENCE

This large picture-postcard *village perché*, draped gently over a hill close to Cagnes, was appointed a 'Royal Town' by King François in the 16th century, and the wealth of the village is still apparent.

In the 1920s St-Paul was discovered by a group of impoverished artists – Signac, Bonnard, Modigliani and Soutine – who stayed at the modest Auberge de la Colombe d'Or, paying for their lodgings with their paintings. Word of the *auberge* spread and soon other artists and intellectuals arrived. Today the exclusive Hôtel La Colombe d'Or boasts an impressive past guest list including Braque, Derain, Matisse, Kipling, Picasso and Utrillo and, as a result, one of the finest private collections of modern art in France.

The village is still an artists' colony, although perhaps better described as a tourist trap, with bus-loads flocking to the Fondation Maeght (➤ 42) and the chic shops and galleries which line its steep, cobbled streets. Despite of the crowds, it remains one of Provence's most exquisite villages.

www.saint-pauldevence.com

➕ 20K 🛈 Maison de la tour, 2 rue Grande ☎ 04 93 32 86 95

TOURRETTES-SUR-LOUP

This 15th-century town is known
as the 'town of violets'. The best
time to visit is in March for the
Fête des Violettes, when the
rose-pink façades of the houses
are smothered in tiny purple
bouquets. They are later distilled
in the regional perfume houses,
crystallized or sold in bouquets
throughout France. The town is
also known for its craft shops.

www.tourrettessurloup.com

19K

2 place de la Libération

04 93 24 18 93

VENCE

Once the Roman forum of
Vintium, this old town became a
bishopric in the Middle Ages, and
its 10th-century cathedral is the
smallest in France. Its interior is
rich in treasures, with Roman
tombstones and a remarkable
Chagall mosaic.

Artists and writers have long
been attracted to the town, just
10km (6.2 miles) from the
crowded coast – including Gide,
Valéry, Dufy and DH Lawrence. In
1941 Henri Matisse moved here,
but soon fell seriously ill.
Dominican sisters nursed him

back to health and, in gratitude, he built and decorated the beautiful **Chapelle du Rosaire** for them. The interior is compelling in its simplicity, with powerful black line-drawings of the Stations of the Cross on white faïence, coloured only by pools of light from the stained-glass windows. Matisse worked on this piece well into his 80s, considering it his 'ultimate goal, the culmination of an intense, sincere and difficult endeavour'.

www.ville-vence.fr

➕ 20K

ℹ place du Grand-Jardin ☎ 04 93 58 06 38

Chapelle du Rosaire

✉ avenue Henri Matisse ☎ 04 93 58 03 26 🕐 Daily 10–11:30, 2–5:30
✋ Inexpensive

VILLENEUVE-LOUBET

Villeneuve-Loubet is dominated by a 33m-high (108ft) pentagonal watchtower, part of an impressive medieval fortress given to the Villeneuves in 1200 by the Count of Provence. The **Musée Militaire** has fascinating displays devoted to 20th-century conflicts.

The village's main attraction, however, is the **Musée de l'Art Culinaire,** created in the home of Auguste Escoffier (1847–1935), the great French 'chef of kings and the king of chefs' who invented the *bombe Néro* and *pêche Melba*. The museum contains all the things one would expect to find in the world's most famous kitchen, including exquisite sugar, chocolate and marzipan work.

www.ot-villeneuveloubet.org

➕ 20K

ℹ 16 avenue de la Mer ☎ 04 93 20 16 16

Musée Militaire

✉ 6 place de Verdun 🕐 Daily 9:30–12, 2–6 ✋ Moderate

Musée de l'Art Culinaire

✉ 1 rue Escoffier ☎ 04 93 20 80 51; www.fondation-escoffier.org
🕐 Sun–Fri 2–6 (7 in summer). Closed Sat, Nov and hols ✋ Inexpensive

HOTELS

ANTIBES
Auberge Provençale (€)
This traditional-style inn offers friendly service and five cosy, comfortable bedrooms overlooking the main square of the old town. Reservations essential.
✉ 61 place Nationale ☎ 04 93 34 13 24

BIOT
Des Arcades (€–€€)
See pages 78–79.

CANNES
Martinez (€€€)
This deluxe hotel contains Cannes' top restaurant, La Palme d'Or – excellent for star-spotting during the Film Festival (➤ 118).
✉ 73 la Croisette ☎ 04 92 98 73 00; www.hotel-marinez.com

Villa de l'Olivier (€€–€€€)
A family-run hotel in Cannes' ancient le Suquet district near the beach and the old port, with 24 rooms, swimming pool and garden with views overlooking Cannes. No restaurant.
✉ 5 rue des Tambourinaires ☎ 04 93 39 53 28; www.hotelolivier.com

FAYENCE
Moulin de la Camandoule (€€€)
See pages 78–79.

Les Oliviers (€€)
A comfortable hotel set in pretty Varois countryside, with a sunny terrace and garden. No restaurant.
✉ quartier Ferrage, route de Grasse, Fayence ☎ 04 94 76 13 12

GRASSE
Hôtel des Parfums (€€)
Ideally situated for visiting Grasse's perfume factories. Ask for a room with a view. After a busy day's sight-seeing, enjoy the

outdoor pool, sauna and hammam.

✉ boulevard Eugène-Charabot ☎ 04 92 42 35 35;
www.hoteldesparfums.com

JUAN-LES-PINS
Le Méridien Garden Beach Hotel (€€€)
Méridien Garden Beach is one of surprisingly few Riviera hotels
actually located right on the beach. This stylish hotel describes
itself as having '*pieds dans l'eau*' (feet in the water).

✉ 15–17 boulevard Baudoin, La Pinède ☎ 04 92 93 57 57;
www.lemeridien-juanlespins.com

LE LAVANDOU
Hotel Les Roches (€€–€€€)
See pages 78–79.

MOUGINS
Le Manoir de l'Étang (€€€)
An intimate manor house, set in 5ha (12 acres) of parkland, with
pool and sun room, a chic restaurant and five golf courses nearby.

✉ 66 allée du Manoir, route d'Antibes ☎ 04 92 28 36 00;
www.manoir-de-letang.com ⏱ Closed Nov–Feb

ST-PAUL-DE-VENCE
La Colombe d'Or (€€€)
Once a modest 1920s café where Braque, Matisse, Picasso and
Léger used to pay for their drinks with canvases. Now a deluxe
hotel. Reserve in advance.

✉ place du Général de Gaulle ☎ 04 93 32 80 02; www.la-colombe-dor.com

La Grande Bastide (€€–€€€)
An 18th-century country house with ten charming Provençal-style
rooms and views of St-Paul. Excellent value. No restaurant.

✉ 1356 route de la Colle ☎ 04 93 32 50 30

Le St-Paul (€€€)
This romantic old 'Relais et Chateaux' hotel, at the heart of the

village, would make a dreamy honeymoon venue.

✉ 86 rue Grande ☎ 04 93 32 65 25; www.lesaintpaul.com

TOURETTES
Four Seasons Resort Provence at Terre Blanche (€€€€)
This exclusive new golf resort near Fayence has been designed to resemble a Provençal village and offers a real getaway from the hustle and bustle of the Riviera.

✉ Domaine de Terre Blanche ☎ 04 94 39 90 00; www.fourseasons.com/provence

VENCE
Le Relais Cantemerle (€€–€€€)
A tranquil oasis in the heart of the Vençoise hills with a pool and excellent restaurant.

✉ 258 chemin Cantemerle ☎ 04 93 58 08 18; www.relais-cantemerle.com
🕐 Open Easter to mid-Oct

RESTAURANTS

ANTIBES
Restaurant de Bacon (€€€€)
One of the coast's best fish restaurants with exceptional views over old Antibes and unforgettable *bouillabaisse*.

✉ boulevard Bacon, Cap d'Antibes ☎ 04 93 61 50 02; www.restaurantdebacon.com 🕐 Closed Mon and Tue lunch (except Jul–Aug) and Nov–Feb

BIOT
Auberge du Jarrier (€€)
Imaginative cuisine and an unmistakably Provençal flavour in an old jar factory.

✉ 30 passage de la Bourgade ☎ 04 93 65 11 68 🕐 Thu–Mon 12–1:30, 7–9:30. Closed Tue and Wed

CANNES
La Palme d'Or (€€€)
Join the stars at Cannes' most prestigious restaurant to

experience the latest culinary creations of prize-winning master chef Christian Willer.

✉ Hôtel Martinez ☎ 04 92 98 74 14 🕐 Closed Mon and Tue out of season

Le Poisson Grillé (€)

This cheap, cheerful restaurant by the old port has specialized in grilled fish dishes for over 50 years, and provides a perfect refuge from the glitz and glamour of Cannes.

✉ 8 quai St Pierre ☎ 04 93 39 44 68; www.poisson-grille.com

La Tarterie (€)

See pages 58–59.

FAYENCE
Le Castelleras (€€€€)

A dish of frogs' legs wrapped in pastry with cream and chives is just one of many local specialties served in this old stone farmhouse.

✉ route de Seillans ☎ 04 94 76 13 80; www.castelleras.com 🕐 Wed–Sun 12–2:30, 7–9:30. Closed Mon–Tue

Le France (€€)

Classic French, candle-lit restaurant in the centre of town with a pretty, flower-fill terrace. Start with *terrine de chèvre*, then *magret de canard* followed by *crème brûlée*.

✉ 1 grande rue de Château ☎ 04 94 76 00 14 🕐 Closed Sun eve and Mon

GRASSE
La Bastide St-Antoine (€€€)

Jacques Chibois – one of the Riviera's top chefs – serves up delectable Provençal cuisine in this auberge, surrounded by olive groves just outside Grasse. Excellent value lunch menu.

✉ 48 av Henri Dunant, Grasse ☎ 04 93 70 94 94; www.jacques-chibois.com

JUAN-LES-PINS
La Bodega (€)

A jolly, family restaurant specializing in wood-fire pizzas, pasta and grills, served with a smile; live music most evenings.

✉ rue Dautheville ☎ 04 93 67 59 02 🕒 Thu–Tue 12–2, 7–10:30

Café de la Plage (€)

Surely the biggest ice creams on the Riviera. Try the aptly named Coupe Mont Blanc or Coupe de la Plage with nougat, honey and pralines. Delicious!

✉ 1 boulevard Baudoin ☎ 04 93 61 37 61

L'Oasis (€€)

See pages 58–59.

LE LAVANDOU

Hotel Les Roches (€€–€€€)

Enjoy inventive regional cuisine, flavoured with herbs from the surrounding hills and accompanied by an excellent wine list.

✉ 1 avenue de trois Dauphins, Aiguebelle plage ☎ 04 94 71 05 07; www.hotellesroches.com

MOUGINS

Le Moulin de Mougins (€€€)

See pages 58–59.

Les Muscadins (€€€)

This restaurant, where an obscure artist called Picasso once stayed, serves delicious regional cuisine with Italian influences.

✉ 19 boulevard Courteline ☎ 04 92 28 28 28 🕒 Daily 12–2, 7:30–9:45. Closed first three weeks in Jan

ST-PAUL-DE-VENCE

Café de la Place (€–€€)

See pages 58–59.

Chez Andreas (€)

A cheerful café-bar on the village ramparts, ideal for lunch or a glass of wine at sunset. Be sure to sample the desserts.

✉ rempart Ouest ☎ 04 93 32 98 32

Le Mas d'Artigny (€€€)

Set in beautiful parkland and part of an exquisite hotel, this gourmet restaurant serves exceptional fish dishes.

✉ route de la Colle ☎ 04 93 32 84 54 🕔 Daily 12–2, 7:30–9:30

SHOPPING

ART AND ANTIQUES

Galerie des Arcades

You will always remember your visit if you buy a print, etching, sculpture or original painting of the Riviera from here.

✉ place aux Arcades, Biot ☎ 04 93 65 10 04

Heidi's English Bookshop

The biggest English-language bookshop on the Côte d'Azur, with a wide choice of new and used books, stationery and cards.

✉ 24 rue Aubernon, Antibes ☎ 04 93 34 74 11 🕔 Daily 10–7

FASHION AND FABRICS

See also pages 72–73.

Fayence Tissu

This fabric shop boasts over 400 different Provençal prints.

✉ 24 place Léon Roux, Fayence ☎ 04 94 76 10 61 🕔 Mon–Sat 9–12:30, 3–7

Legend

Young, trendy designs for the seriously fashionable here include French Connection, Kenzo, Moschino and Caterpillar labels.

✉ boulevard Baudoin, Galerie Eden Beach, Juan-les-Pins ☎ 04 93 67 33 55
🕔 Daily 10:30–12:30, 2:30–6

Naf-Naf

Brightly coloured, sporty fashions for men, women and children.

✉ 1 boulevard Baudoin, Juan-les-Pins ☎ 04 93 61 26 97; www.nafnaf.com
🕔 Daily 10–1, 3–7

FOOD AND DRINK

Ceneri

One of France's leading cheese stores with over 300 varieties –
from huge rounds of runny brie to tiny *boutons de culotte*
(trouser-button) goat cheese.

✉ 22 rue Meynadier, Cannes ☎ 04 93 99 23 05

Olives – Les Huiles du Monde

You'll find everything imaginable here that's produced with olives
from Provence and the Mediterranean, ranging from delicious olive
oils and tapenades to soaps and cosmetics.

✉ 68 rue Grande ☎ 04 90 92 53 93 🕔 Daily 9:30-7

La Petite Cave de Saint-Paul

An authentic 14th-century cellar containing a choice selection of
Provençal wines, including those produced in the surrounding
vineyards.

✉ 7 rue de l'Etoile, St-Paul-de-Vence ☎ 04 93 32 59 54 🕔 Daily 10–7

L'Univers du Vin

See pages 66–67.

GIFTS AND SOUVENIRS

Antibes Shipservices

You'll find everything nautical here from 'boaty' keyrings to
fashionable yachting gear.

✉ 12 boulevard Aguillon, Antibes ☎ 04 93 34 68 00; www.antibes-ship.com
🕔 Mon–Sat 8:30–12:15, 2–6:15

Dany

Dazzling displays of hand-painted glassware in a tiny atelier,
including lamps, bottles, jars and vases.

✉ 1 bis rue du Mitan, Fayence ☎ 04 94 76 19 85 🕔 Mon–Sat 10:30–12:30,
3:30–7

Geneviéve Lethu

This delightful gift shop is crammed from floor to ceiling with

presents and home decorations and furnishings.
✉ 6 rue Maréchal Joffre, Cannes ☎ 04 93 68 18 19;
www.genevievelethu.com ◷ Daily 9:30–7

Herbier de Provence
See page 66.

Mélonie
Quite simply the most exquisite dried flower arrangements you
are ever likely to see.
✉ 80 rue d'Antibes, Cannes ☎ 04 93 68 60 60 ◷ Daily 10–1, 2–7

L'Occitane
All-natural fragrances, soaps and skincare products embracing the
scents, colours and traditions of Provence.
✉ 14 rue Maréchal Joffre, Cannes ☎ 04 93 68 20 32; www.loccitane.com
◷ Mon–Sat 10–1, 2–7, Sun 10–1

Parfumerie Fragonard
See pages 66–67.

Poterie Provencale
Biot is famed for its pottery and this beautiful shop displays
earthenware pots of every shape and size, rustic garden pots and
terracotta ornaments.
✉ 1689 route de la Mer, Biot ☎ 04 93 65 63 30

Verrerie de Biot
See page 66.

Les Volets Blancs
Luxurious handmade throws, quilts and beautiful hand-
embroidered linens for the home.
✉ 1 rue des Bauques ☎ 04 93 32 56 47; www.les-volets-blancs.com
◷ Summer 10:15–12:30, 2.15–7pm; winter 10:15–12:30, 2.15–6:30pm

ENTERTAINMENT

Espace Miramar

A popular theatre venue, featuring classical and modern productions, and films during the International Film Festival.

✉ Palais Miramar, 65 boulevard Croisette, Cannes ☎ 04 93 43 86 26

La Siesta

See pages 62-63

Whisky à Gogo

Join the locals for the latest sounds in this overflowingly popular nightclub.

✉ rue Jacques Leonetti, Juan-les-Pins ☎ 04 93 61 26 40 ⏰ Daily from 10:30pm

SPORTS

Centre Nautique Municipal de Cannes

Classes in sailing dinghies and catamarans, and surf-boarding for adults and children.

✉ Port du Mouvré Rouge, Cannes ☎ 04 92 18 88 87

Club Alpin François

Rock and ice cascade climbing expeditions.

✉ 87 boulevard Carnot, Cannes ☎ 04 93 68 46 17

Golf Club Cannes-Mandelieu Riviera

One of the largest golf courses in Europe.

✉ route du Golf, 06210 Mandelieu-la Napoule ☎ 04 92 97 49 49

Guigo Marine, Antibes

Tired of lazing on the beach? Book a day trip and try your hand at deep-sea fishing.

✉ 9 avenue 11-Novembre ☎ 04 93 34 17 17 ⏰ Jun–Oct

Monaco and the Southeast Coast

Monaco

This dramatic stretch of vivid blue coastline with its chic cities, sandy beaches, craggy corniches and fishing villages has long attracted a rich assortment of actors, artists, writers and royalty to its shores. After all, this is the home of the rich and famous – the world's most sophisticated holiday playground.

Nowhere is the affluence of the Riviera more apparent than in the tiny Principality of Monaco, with its luxury high-rise hotels, designer shops and ports overflowing with millionaires' yachts. The neighbouring resort of Cap Ferrat is nicknamed the 'Peninsula of Billionaires' with its ostentatious villas set in subtropical gardens, while nearby Villefranche-sur-Mer remains chic but

surprisingly unspoilt with its picturesque natural harbour.

If it weren't for the steep cliffs that plunge down to the sea between Nice and Menton, it would be easy to forget that 80 per cent of the Alpes-Maritimes is composed of mountains. The Corniches between Nice and Menton offer drivers some breath-taking scenery and the entire area is scattered with timeless villages, from remote Peille and Peillon dozing in the hinterland to Èze, a spectacular hilltop village which clings to a cliff edge above the azure sea.

MONACO

The Principality of Monaco is the world's second smallest sovereign state after the Vatican – a 195ha (481 acres), spotlessly clean skyscraper-clad strip squeezed between sea and mountains on largely reclaimed land. It is a magnet for the world's jet-setters, attracted by the lack of taxes and the world's highest incomes.

Only 7,000 of Monaco's 32,000 residents are Monégasque. The remainder are all prepared to pay exorbitant prices for a cramped high-rise apartment in order to be part of Monaco's famed community of millionaires, gamblers and 'offshore' bankers.

With so much evident wealth and glamour, it is hard to imagine Monaco's turbulent past. At various times occupied by the French, the Spanish and the Dukes of Savoy, for over 700 years the principality has been ruled by the Grimaldi family, the world's oldest reigning monarchy, in power ever since 1297 when a Grimaldi known as Francesco 'the Spiteful' dressed up as a friar and knocked at the door of Monaco's Ghibelline fortress asking for hospitality, together with his men, disguised as monks. Once inside, they killed the guards and took control of the garrison. Hence the sword-brandishing monks on the Grimaldi family crest.

The Grimaldis once ruled an area which extended along the coast from Antibes to Menton. However, their high taxes provoked a revolt, and the principality shrank to its present size. In the mid-19th century, Prince Charles III of Monaco, facing a financial crisis, opened the Casino to increase revenue. It was such a success that taxes were soon abolished altogether. Charles was succeeded by Prince Albert I, who introduced numerous academic and scientific institutions, including the Musée Océanographique (► 50). From

1949 until his death in 2005, Monaco was ruled by Prince Rainier Louis Henri Maxence Bertrand de Grimaldi who invested considerably in modernising the principality.

In 1956, Prince Rainier added fairy-tale cachet to his realm by marrying the legendary American film star Grace Kelly, who met with a tragic car accident in 1982 along la Moyenne Corniche. Their son Albert is the current ruler, making him the Riviera's most sought-after bachelor, although Stéphanie and Caroline, his sometimes wayward sisters, tend to dominate the press.

Even though Monaco is so small, finding your way around can prove difficult. Not only is Monaco the name of the principality, but Monaco-Ville is also a district on the peninsula to the south, containing the old town with its narrow streets. By startling contrast, the newer high-rise district of Monte-Carlo to the east is centred round the Casino and designer shops. The port quarter, between the districts of Monte-Carlo and Monaco-Ville, is called la Condamine, and there is an industrial district, Fontvieille, to the southwest.

www.monaco-tourisme.com

✚ 22K

ℹ️ 2a boulevard des Moulins, Monte Carlo ☎ 377/92 16 61 16

Casino

Best places to see ➤ 36–37.

Cathédrale

Built in 1875 (and funded by Casino profits), this ostentatious neo-Romanesque cathedral has among its treasures two 16th-century retables by Niçoise artist Louis Bréa, and the tomb of the still much-mourned Princess Grace.

✉️ 4 rue Colonel Bellando de Castro, Monaco-Ville ☎ 377/93 30 87 70

🕐 Daily 7am–7pm 🚌 1, 2 💷 Free

La Condamine

In medieval times, la Condamine referred to arable land at the foot of a village or a castle. Today this area, at the foot of the royal palace is a busy commercial district wrapped around the port of Monaco. It is fun to wander along the quayside, to marvel at the size and cost of the yachts, but take time to explore the back streets too, for they hide some superb shops and restaurants.

🚌 1, 2, 4, 5, 6 🛥 Apr–Sep daily excursions round the Rock, or further afield to Îles de Lérins, St-Tropez or San Remo in Italy ✉ quai des Etats-Unis Port d'Hercule (Aquavision boat trips ☎ 377/92 16 15 15; www.aquavision-monaco.com)

Fontvieille

This zone of modern residential and commercial development, built on reclaimed land below the rock of Monaco-Ville, has a marina, sports stadium and excellent shops; it also has a fine park, and the Princess Grace Rose Garden, a peaceful oasis fragrant with the scent of 4,000 rose trees.

The terraces of Fontvieille were specially built to house numerous museums, including Prince Rainier's private **collection of classic cars,** a **Naval Museum,** with 180 models of famous ships, a stamp and coin museum, and even a zoo.

Collection de Voitures
☎ 377/92 05 28 56 🕐 Daily 10–6 💵 Moderate 🚌 5, 6
Musée Naval
☎ 377/92 05 28 48; www.musee-naval.mc 🕐 Daily 10–6 💵 Moderate
🚌 5, 6

Jardin Exotique de Moneghetti

Just off the Moyenne Corniche, above Fontvieille, lies one of Monaco's finest attractions, the **Exotic Garden,** containing several thousand cacti and succulents of vivid colours and amazing shapes (some nearly 10m/33ft high).

🕐 16 Sep–14 May 9–6 (or until nightfall). Closed 19 Nov 💵 Moderate 🚌 2

Monaco-Ville

The labyrinth of cool, cobbled streets perched on 'the Rock' (a sheer-sided finger of land extending 800m/2625ft into the sea) has been well preserved, with lovely fountain-filled squares and fine Italianate façades – although, inevitably, the shops around the royal palace purvey the usual tacky souvenirs. Look for the multi-screen **Monte-Carlo Story** and the fascinating **Musée du Vieux Monaco,** portraying life on the Rock throughout the centuries. The Historial des Princes de Monaco depicts historical episodes in the Grimaldi dynasty through life-sized wax models.

Monte-Carlo Story

✉ terrasses du parking du Chemin des Pêcheurs ☎ 377/93 25 32 33 🕙 Jan–Jun, Sep–Oct daily hourly 35 min programmes 2–5, Jul–Aug 2–6 👆 Expensive 🚌 1, 2

Musée du Vieux Monaco

✉ rue Emile de Loth ☎ 377/93 50 57 28 🕙 Open by appointment 👆 Free 🚌 1, 2

Musée Océanographique

Best places to see ➤ 50–51.

Palais du Prince

Guided tours take visitors through the treasures of the state apartments and the small Musée Napoléon in the south wing of the palace, when Prince Albert is away. When he is in residence, the royal colours are flown from the tower, and visitors must be content with the changing of the guard ceremony which is held every morning at 11:55.

✉ place du Palais ☎ 377/93 25 18 31; www.palais.mc 🕙 Jun–Sep 9:30–6:30; Oct 10–5:30. Closed Nov–May 👆 Moderate 🚌 1, 2

a drive from Monaco

The D53 zigzags for 6km (3.7 miles) high above Monaco to la Turbie.

La Turbie is easily recognizable due to the huge Roman monument, the Trophée des Alpes, built in honour of Emperor Augustus, who captured this region in the 1st century BC.

Exit la Turbie on the D53 (direction Peille). The road winds inland through wild countryside to Peille.

Peille (➤ 152) is full of surprises: ancient mansions redolent of a noble past; attractive squares adorned with Gothic fountains, arches and urns; even an old salt-tax office.

Backtrack south, along the D53 again. Turn left along the D22 through barren garrigue scrub, over the Col de La Madone and through a small forest to Ste-Agnès.

At 650m (2133ft), Ste-Agnès is the highest village on the Riviera, and rated 'one of the most beautiful villages in France'.

Take the D22 towards Menton. Immediately after crossing the autoroute, take a tiny unsignposted lane on the right (the Chemin des Vignes) to Gorbio.

The best time to visit medieval Gorbio is in June, when the Snail Festival takes place and the streets are lit with thousands of tiny lamps made from snail shells.

Leave Gorbio along avenue Aristide Briand (signed Grande Corniche). Turn left on to the D2564 to Roquebrune old village (➤ 154).

Don't miss the splendid view from Roquebrune castle's terrace over sloping orange roofs past dark cypress trees to the sparkling sea beyond.

Return on the D2564 toward la Turbie. Turn left after Hôtel Le Vista Palace (D51) and on to Monaco via the RN7.

Distance 66km (41 miles)
Time Allow a full day including visits
Start/end point Monaco ✚ 22K
Lunch La Vieille Auberge (€)
✉ Ste-Agnès ☎ 04 93 35 92 02

More to see on the Southeast Coast

BEAULIEU-SUR-MER

Beaulieu really is a 'beautiful place' and one of the warmest resorts on the Riviera, sheltered by a natural amphitheatre of hills. It had its heyday at the turn of the century when many celebrities stayed here, including the Prince of Wales, Empress Sissi of Austria, Pyotr Ilyich Tchaikovsky and Gustav Eiffel. It still boasts many attractions, including an elegant palm-lined promenade, a glamorous casino, the elegant Edwardian Rotonde and the extraordinary **Villa Kérylos.**

This seaside villa was built by archaeologist Théodore Reinach in 1908 as a tribute to life in ancient Greece. No expense was spared in its lavish décor of white, yellow and lavender marble, ivory and bronze. Reinach lived here for almost 20 years, eating, dressing and behaving as an Athenian citizen.

➕ 22K

ℹ place Clemenceau ☎ 04 93 01 02 21

Villa Kérylos

✉ Impasse Eiffel ☎ 04 93 01 01 42

🕐 6 Nov to mid-Feb Mon–Fri 2–6, Sat–Sun 10–6; mid-Feb to 5 Nov 10–6 (until 7 Jul–Aug) ✋ Expensive

CAP FERRAT

The most desirable address on the Riviera – the 'Peninsula of Billionaires' – has long been a favourite haunt of the rich and famous, including Somerset Maugham, Edith Piaf, Charlie Chaplin and David Niven.

The cape is smothered in huge villas hidden among

sumptuous gardens, including the Villa des Cèdres – one of Europe's most beautiful private botanical gardens, with 12,000 species of exotic plants – and the peninsula's finest property, Villa Ephrussi de Rothschild (► 54). A shaded coastal path from Villefranche around the cape past countless enticing inlets makes a pleasant stroll before lunch in St-Jean-Cap-Ferrat.

✚ 22K

🔒 59 av Denis Semeria, 06230 St-Jean-Cap-Ferrat ☎ 04 93 76 08 90

LES CORNICHES

Three famous cliff roads, called la Grande Corniche (D2564), la Moyenne Corniche (N7) and l'Inférieure Corniche, traverse the scenic and most mountainous stretch of the Riviera from Nice to Menton via Monaco.

They each zigzag their way along vertiginous ledges at three different heights. The highest road – la Grande Corniche – was originally constructed by Napoléon and is by far the best choice for picnickers and nature lovers. The lowest route (l'Inférieure) follows the coastal contours through all the seaside resorts, and is best avoided during July and August. The steep Moyenne at the middle level is the most dramatic. It was on this cliff hanging route, with its hair-raising bends and astounding views, that Grace Kelly met her untimely death in 1982. Today the road is frequently used for filming car chases.

✚ 22K

ÈZE

Best places to see ► 40–41.

MENTON

Until the mid-19th century, when the Riviera became a fashionable and wealthy winter resort, Menton was a little-known fishing port belonging to the Grimaldis. *Fin de siècle* hotels resembling palaces started to spring up throughout the town. After WW I, Menton lost out to its more glamorous neighbours – Nice, Cannes, St-Tropez and Monaco – although its faded elegance is still apparent.

The medieval old town is a hotchpodge of ancient pastel-coloured houses, alleys and tiny squares. There are two baroque churches: St-Michel and the Chapelle de la Conception, with ornamented façades. Between them, the Parvis St-Michel, a mosaic square of black and white cobbles depicting the Grimaldi coat of arms, provides the setting for the Chamber Music Festival.

On the site of the ancient castle at the top of the old town, a fascinating cemetery with sweeping views reflects the cosmopolitanism of the town at the end of the last century. Other notable sights include the **Musée de la Préhistoire Régional, Palais Carnolès,** the 18th-century summer residence of the Princes of Monaco, now Menton's main art museum; and the **Musée Jean Cocteau,** dedicated to the town's most famous son. Cocteau also decorated the remarkable **Salle des Mariages** in the Hôtel de Ville with romantic, spiritual and ironic images.

Menton is France's warmest town, boasting an annual 300 days of sun and as a result the town is bursting with semi-tropical gardens. Most of them are in the wealthy Garavan district in the foothills behind the town, notably the Jardin Botanique, the ancient olive grove of Parc du Pian and the Valencian Jardin Fontana Rosa.

Menton is also the 'lemon capital of the world', and the terraced slopes behind are covered in citrus groves. The Biovès garden in the town centre is the venue in February of Menton's spectacular *Fête du Citron* (www.feteducitron.com).

www.menton.fr

✚ 23L ❓ Ten-day Lemon Festival *(Fête du Citron)* in Feb; Music Festival in Aug

ℹ️ Palais de l'Europe, 8 avenue Boyer ☎ 04 92 41 76 76

Musée de la Préhistoire Régional

✉️ rue Lorédan Larchey ☎ 04 93 35 84 64 🕐 Wed–Mon 10–12, 2–6. Closed Tue and hols 💷 Free

Palais Carnolès Musée des Beaux-Arts

✉️ 3 avenue de la Madone ☎ 04 93 35 49 71 🕐 Wed–Mon 10–12. 2–6. Closed Tue and hols 💷 Free ❓ Free access also to the citrus gardens

Musée Jean Cocteau

✉️ Baston du Vieux Port quai Napoléon III ☎ 04 93 57 72 30 🕐 Wed–Mon 10–12, 2–6. Closed Tue and hols 💷 Inexpensive

Salle des Mariages

✉️ 17 rue de la Républik ☎ 04 92 10 50 11 🕐 Mon–Fri 8:30–12, 1:30–5. Closed Sat, Sun and hols 💷 Inexpensive

PEILLE

Just a short distance inland and set in wild, underpopulated countryside, Peille is a perfect retreat from the touristic frenzy of the coast, a unique hilltop village, with its own Provençal dialect, *Pelhasc*.

Peille had unusual ideas on religion too. During the Middle Ages, it was excommunicated several times rather than pay the bishop's tithes. The Chapelle des Pénitents Noirs was converted into a communal oil press and its splendid domed Chapelle de St-Sébastien into the Hôtel de Ville.

Inside the church of Ste-Marie is an interesting painting of the village in medieval times, showing the now-ruined castle in its former glory. Once, during a drought, Peille asked a local shepherd for help. He made it rain on condition that the lord of the castle agreed to give him his daughter's hand in marriage – an event still celebrated on the first Sunday in September.

✚ 22L ❓ Ask for the key to the church of Ste-Marie at the hospice

ℹ Mairie ☎ 04 93 91 71 71

PEILLON

Peille's twin and neighbouring village, Peillon is one of the Riviera's most beautiful hilltop village, very cleverly camouflaged against the landscape. Medieval perched villages were built in lofty positions for safety. From behind their thick ramparts, villagers could keep vigil over the hinterland as well as the coast.

Peillon's huddle of cobbled alleys, steps and arches lead up to a charming little church at the summit. But the main attraction here is the Chapelle des Pénitents Blancs just outside the village, with 15th-century frescoes by Giovanni Canavesio depicting the Passion of Christ. Beyond the chapel, a footpath walk to Peille takes about two hours along what was once a Roman road.

✚ 22L ❓ Call in advance to arrange a visit to the Chapelle des Pénitents Blancs ℹ Mairie ☎ 04 93 79 91 04

ROQUEBRUNE-CAP-MARTIN

Located on a prime site between Menton and Monaco, Roquebrune-Cap-Martin is divided into two areas: old Roquebrune, an attractive medieval hilltop village and the stylishcoastal resort of Cap Martin.

Old Roquebrune is a fascinating tangle of ancient lanes, stairways and vaulted passages clustered around its castle, the oldest feudal château remaining in France and the sole example of Carolingian style. Built in the 10th century to ward off Saracen attack, it was later remodelled by the Grimaldis, and restored in 1911 by Lord Ingram, one of the first wave of wealthy tourist residents drawn to Cap Martin.

Other visitors attracted to Cap Martin included Queen Victoria, Coco Chanel and architect Le Corbusier, who drowned off the cape in 1965 and lies buried in Roquebrune cemetery. A delightful coastal path in his honour (promenade Le Corbusier) circles the cape.

www.roquebrune-cap-martin.com

✚ 23L 🅿 Food and flower market daily

🛈 218 av Aristide Briand ☎ 04 93 35 62 87

VILLA EPHRUSSI DE ROTHSCHILD

Best places to see ➤ 54–55.

VILLEFRANCHE-SUR-MER

Villefranche remains surprisingly unspoiled, considering its proximity to Nice and Monte-Carlo. Indeed, it has changed little since it was founded in the 14th century as a customs-free port.

Its beautiful deep bay is fringed with red and orange Italianate houses and atmospheric waterfront bars, cafés and restaurants.

A cobweb of steep stairways and passageways climb from the harbour through the old town. The narrow, vaulted rue Obscure has sheltered the inhabitants of Villefranche from bombardments throughout history right up to World War II.

The sturdy 16th-century citadel on the waterfront contains galleries with work by local artists, including Picasso and Miró. On the quay, the 14th-century **Chapelle St-Pierre,** once used to store fishing nets, was decorated in 1957 with frescoes by Jean Cocteau.

www.villefranche-sur-mer.com

✚ 21K 🛈 Jardin François Binon ☎ 04 93 01 73 68

Chapelle St-Pierre

✉ Quai Courbet, Port de Villefranche ☎ 04 93 76 90 70 🕓 Tue–Sun 9:30–12, 3–7 💲 Inexpensive

HOTELS

BEAULIEU-SUR-MER
La Réserve (€€€)
One of the most exclusive seafront hotels of the Riviera, with an elegant and formal atmosphere.
✉ 5 boulevard Maréchal-Leclerc ☎ 04 93 01 00 01; www.reservebeaulieu.com

ÈZE
Château Èza (€€€)
See pages 78–79.

MENTON
Des Ambassadeurs (€€€)
Menton's top hotel boasts all the facilities you would expect and a prime location in the centre of town but, surprisingly, no pool.
✉ 3 rue Partouneaux ☎ 04 93 28 75 75; www.ambassadeurs-menton.com

Pension Beauregard (€)
A small, friendly hotel with pretty gardens in the centre of town.
✉ 10 rue Albert 1er, Menton ☎ 04 93 28 63 63

MONACO
L'Hermitage (€€€)
See pages 78–79.

Hôtel de France (€€)
Hôtel de France is one of the few affordable hotels in the principality – cheap and cheerful and situated near the station.
✉ 6 rue de la Turbie, Monte-Carlo ☎ 377/93 30 24 64

Hôtel de Paris (€€€)
Aristocrats and gamblers have frequented Monte-Carlo's most prestigious address for over 100 years. Facilities include a fine swimming pool, garden and a rooftop restaurant.
✉ place du Casino, Monte-Carlo ☎ 377/98 06 30 00; www.montecarloresort.com

PEILLON
Auberge de la Madone (€€)
This typical auberge has been lovingly decorated in traditional Provençal style. Balmy evenings are spent on the restaurant terrace, enjoying the establishment's delicious home cooking.
✉ 3 place Auguste Arnulf ☎ 04 93 79 91 17 🕐 Closed Oct–Jan

ROQUEBRUNE-CAP-MARTIN
Vista Palace (€€€)
Don't be put off by this ugly, modern building, perched on a 300m-high (984ft) cliff on the Grande Corniche overlooking Monaco, for inside you will find the ultimate in luxury.
✉ 1551 route Turbie, Grande Corniche ☎ 04 92 10 40 00; www.vistapalace.com

ST-JEAN-CAP-FERRAT
Clair Logis (€€)
This simple villa hotel is set in a large garden, on a quiet street at the heart of the wooded peninsula. Excellent for those who seek the elegance of the Cap without the prices. No restaurant.
✉ 12 avenue Prince Rainier III de Monaco ☎ 04 93 76 51 81; www.hotel-clair-logis.fr

RESTAURANTS

ÈZE
La Bergerie (€€)
Traditional dishes with a good choice of Côtes de Provence wines. Dine in winter by the welcoming open fire, and in summer on the shady terrace overlooking the sea.
✉ RN7 ☎ 04 93 41 03 67 🕐 Eves only; weekends only in winter

Le Cactus (€)
This delightful, vaulted restaurant in Èze's old gateway serves cheap but tasty crêpes.
✉ La Placette, entrée Vieux Village, Èze ☎ 04 93 41 19 02 🕐 Mar–Oct 9–9; in winter only open at weekends and school holidays. Closed Jan

La Chèvre d'Or (€€€)

Inspiring French cuisine in a magnificent medieval castle-hotel with breathtaking sea views to match.

✉ 3 rue du Barri ☎ 04 92 10 66 66; www.chevredor.com ⏰ Closed Nov to mid-Mar

MENTON
Don Cicco (€)

Italian cuisine less than a kilometre from the Italian border.

✉ 11 rue St-Michel ☎ 04 93 57 92 92 ⏰ Thu–Tue 12–2, 7–10

L'Olivo (€€)

This cosy restaurant at the foot of the old town serves giant pizzas from an open oven along with mouth-watering *moules frites* or beef *carpaccio à discretion*.

✉ 21 place du Cap ☎ 04 93 35 45 65 ⏰ Daily 12–2, 6:45–10:30

Au Pistou (€€)

Regional and delicous Mentonnaise specialities beside the old fishing harbour.

✉ 9 quai Gordon Bennett ☎ 04 93 57 45 89 ⏰ Tue–Sun 12:15–1:30, 7:30–9:30

MONACO
Castelroc (€€)

This crowded and popular lunch spot opposite the Prince's palace has been run by the same family for over 50 years and serves exceptional Monégasque cuisine.

✉ place du Palais, Monaco-ville ☎ 377/93 30 36 68 ⏰ Closed Sat and Dec

Louis XV (€€€)

Should you break the bank at the Casino, come to the Louis XV to blow your winnings. The lunch menu is excellent value.

✉ Hôtel de Paris, place du Casino, Monte Carlo ☎ 377/98 06 88 64; www.alain-ducasse.com ⏰ Closed Tue, Wed Nov–27 Dec and 24 Feb–10 Mar

Polpetta (€€)

Hidden away from the clamour of central Monte-Carlo, this vivacious Italian restaurant nonetheless attracts jet-setters and celebrities for a taste of *la dolce vita*.

✉ 6 avenue de Rocqueville, Monte Carlo ☎ 377/93 50 67 84 🕐 Closed Tue, and Sat lunch

The Waterfront (€€)

This chic restaurant by the port at Fontvieille, serves sensational Mediterranean fish dishes in attractive garden surroundings.

✉ 28 quai Jean-Charles Rey ☎ 377/92 05 90 99 🕐 Daily 12:15–2, 7:30–11

Zebra Square (€€)

See pages 58–59.

ROQUEBRUNE-CAP-MARTIN
Le Grand Inquisiteur (€€€)

These cave-like, vaulted dining-rooms were once used to shelter livestock. Today they make the perfect setting for a candle-lit dinner *à deux*.

✉ rue du Château ☎ 04 93 35 05 37 🕐 Daily 12–2, 7–10 (10:30pm Fri–Sun). Closed Mon and Tue lunch

La Grotte (€)

Feeling peckish? Then tuck into the *plat du jour* at 'the Cave', a popular troglodyte restaurant at the entrance to the village.

✉ place des Deux-Frères ☎ 04 93 35 00 04 🕐 Thu–Mon 12:15–2:30, 7.15–10. Closed Tue pm and Wed

VILLEFRANCHE
La Mère Germaine (€€€€)

One of the most popular waterfront seafood restaurants in Villefranche. Menus change daily depending on the catch.

✉ 7 quai Courbet ☎ 04 93 01 71 39; www.meregermaine.com

SHOPPING

FASHION
La Botterie
See pages 72–73.

Cravatterie Nazionali
A great selection of designer ties.
✉ 17 avenue Spélugues, Monaco ☎ 377/93 50 88 80 🕐 Mon–Sat 10–7:30

Diesel
This popular clothing chain produces casual, affordable clothing for men and women.
✉ 15 rue Grimaldi, la Condamine, Monaco ☎ 377/93 50 34 14;
www.diesel.com 🕐 Mon–Sat 10–12:15, 1–7:15

Hermès
See pages 72–73.

Replay
Vast arrays of smart, trendy jeans, sweaters, shirts, jackets, shoes and accessories for men, women and children – Replay's motto states 'If you can't find it in our store, you don't need it!'
✉ 17 avenue des Spélugues, Galerie Le Métropole, Monte-Carlo ☎ 377/93 25 30 40 🕐 Mon–Sat 10–7:30

Society Club
Men will love this stylish, macho shop, fitted out with wood and leather, selling the latest in labels such as D&G, Boss, YSL and Gucci.
✉ Centre Commercial le Métropole, Monte-Carlo ☎ 377/93 25 25 01
🕐 Mon–Sat 10–7:30

FOOD AND DRINK
Les Caves du Grand Échanson
Suppliers of exclusive wines and spirits to Prince Albert.
✉ 7 rue de la Colle, Monte-Carlo, Monaco ☎ 377/92 05 61 01

DOC D'Italia

No need to cross the border to stock up on Italian goodies. This little store has everything from *panettone* to *pecorino*.

✉ 7 rue Piéta, Menton ☎ 04 92 09 15 40

La Cigale

Try the local speciality, *tarte au citron* (lemon tart) at this delightful pastry shop, made using fruit from the patron's own garden.

✉ 27 avenue Carnot, Menton ☎ 04 93 35 74 66

L'Oenothèque

An old wood-panelled store which stocks fine cognacs, armagnacs and French wines from 1928–2003.

✉ Sporting Club d'Hiver, 2 avenue Princesse Alice, Monte-Carlo, Monaco ☎ 377/93 25 82 66

GIFTS AND SOUVENIRS

Coutellerie E Garnero

This 100-year-old shop specializes in the unlikely combination of knives and umbrellas – surely one of the most old-fashioned, eccentric shops on the Riviera.

✉ 8 rue St-Michel, Menton ☎ 04 93 57 03 60 🕔 Thu–Sat and Mon–Tue 9–12, 2:30–7.

L'Herminette Ezasque

Situated within the walls of Èze's old gateway, this little shop is bursting with *santons* (French figurines), Christmas crib figures and gifts and sculptures made from olive wood.

✉ 1 rue Principale, Èze ☎ 04 93 41 13 59 🕔 Mon–Sat 10–6, Sun 3–6

Manufacture de Monaco

A small, exclusive shop which supplies Monaco's royal family with traditional Monégasque porcelain, silverware, crystal and table linen.

✉ Centre Comerciale le Métropole, 4 avenue de la Madone, Monte-Carlo, Monaco ☎ 377/93 50 64 63; www.mdpm.com 🕔 Mon–Sat 10–7:30

Marie Dentelle

An Aladdin's cave of feminine gift ideas, brightly coloured local pottery, and beautiful bed linen, including amazing handmade quilts made in traditional Provençal material.

✉ 10 rue Princesse Caroline, la Condamine, Monaco ☎ 377/93 30 43 40
🕐 10–7

ENTERTAINMENT

Café de Paris

Even if you are not a big spender, you will be tempted by the dazzling array of slot-machines in this famous café.

✉ place du Casino, Monte-Carlo, Monaco ☎ 377/92 16 20 20
🕐 Daily 10am–2am

Cinema d'Été

See pages 62–63.

Jimmi'z

See pages 62–63.

The Living Room

Piano bar and disco, in the centre of Monte-Carlo.

✉ 7 avenue des Spélugues, Monte-Carlo, Monaco ☎ 377/93 50 80 31
🕐 Mon–Sat 11pm–6am

Salle Garnier

This world-famous opera house, designed by Charles Garnier, architect of the Paris Opéra. Salle Garnier has played host to many great artists over the years.

✉ place du Casino, Monaco ☎ 377/98 06 28 00; www.opera.mc

Le Sporting

Monaco's main cinema complex, inside an arcade with stylish shops, with three screens showing films in their original language.

✉ place du Casino, Monte-Carlo ☎ 08 92 68 0072,
www.cinemasporting.com

St-Tropez and the Southwest Coast

St-Tropez

This stretch of Riviera coastline is wild and rugged with deserted creeks and bleached beaches, far less developed than its eastern counterpart. Its resorts are strung out like pearls along the coast, with St-Tropez the jewel in the crown. No name evokes the *joie de vivre* of the region as much as St'Trop' ('too much') – a hedonistic, 'see-and-be-seen' resort and the home of the bikini –

with its picturesque old port, decadent yachts and glamorous sun-soaked beaches.

Further along the coast, the Corniche de l'Esterel pierces the blood-red cliffs of the seashore with minute inlets, and tiny deserted beaches, while the remarkable remains at Fréjus bear witness to an exceptional heritage as the oldest Roman city in Gaul. Inland, away from the tourist-courting coastal resorts, is some of the most wooded countryside in France. It is a region of wild, unexplored landscapes, its sombre green forests of chestnuts, cork oaks and conifers, interrupted only by an occasional yellow splash of mimosa or a hidden village, drenched in bougainvillea and oleander. It is here, in such slumbering villages as Bormes-les-Mimosas, Grimaud and Collobrieres, that visitors can sample the true 'good life' of rural Provence.

ST-TROPEZ

This charming fishing port, which reached the height of
international fame in the 'swinging' sixties, continues to attract
the rich and famous. Although its hedonistic image has become a
little stale, it remains one of the most seductive resorts of the
entire Riviera.

It is fun to rub shoulders with the glitterati in the waterfront
cafés, and to wonder at the grandiose yachts moored before the
distinctive backdrop of pink and yellow pastel-hued houses,
reconstructed after being destroyed in 1944. But take time to
explore the maze of narrow streets and squares of old St-Tropez,
where there is a village-like atmosphere with markets, chic
boutiques and bistros.

The town has long been a popular meeting place for artists.
Liszt and de Maupassant were its first celebrities in the 1880s,
followed by the painter Signac a decade later. Soon the works of
Matisse, Bonnard, Utrillo and Dufy were to immortalize the town
on canvas. Painters were followed by an influx of writers between
the wars – Colette, Cocteau and Anaïs Nin. Then in the 1950s it
was the turn of the film stars, led by the famous Tropezienne,

Brigitte Bardot, whose film *Et Dieu Créa La Femme* (1956) marked the start of a new, permissive era.

St-Tropez' star-studded list of residents includes Elton John, Jean-Paul Belmondo and Jean Michel Jarre and, everything here continues to be extravagant and decadent. Little wonder the French endearingly call it St 'Trop' ('too much').
www.ot-st-tropez.com

✚ 9D ⛴ Motorboat services run around St-Tropez bay and to Port-Grimaud, Ste-Maxime, les Issambres, St-Raphaël, Cannes and the Îles de Lérins

ℹ quai Jean Jaurès ☎ 04 94 97 45 21

Beaches

St-Tropez owes much of its attraction to its gorgeous sandy beaches, for it was here that girls first dared to bathe topless in the 1960s. In total, there is over 6km (4 miles) of enticing golden sand situated on the Baie de Pampelonne, neatly divided into individual beaches, each with a different character. In summer there's a frequent minibus to the bay from place des Lices.

Les Graniers is the most crowded beach and within easy walking distance of the village; trendy **Club 55** caters for the Paris set; **Tahiti Plage** was once the movie stars' favourite (the original beach bar was constructed from an old film set), but nowadays star-spotters have more luck at the frivolous **Voile Rouge.** For privacy and seclusion, Plage de la Briande is considered by many to be the best beach in the region, situated halfway along the 19km (12 miles) coastal path that rounds the St-Tropez peninsula.

Les Graniers

✉ plage des Graniers ☎ 04 94 97 30 50

Club 55

✉ boulevard Patch ☎ 04 94 55 55 55

Tahiti Plage

✉ route de Tahiti ☎ 04 94 97 18 02

Voile Rouge

✉ route des Tamaris ☎ 04 94 79 84 34

La Citadelle

It is worth visiting this 16th-century hilltop fortress for the view alone, which embraces the orange curved-tile roofs of St-Tropez' old town, the dark and distant Maures and Esterel hills, and the shimmering blue of the bay, flecked with sails. The maritime museum in the citadel keep is an annexe of the Musée de la Marine in the Palais de Chaillot in Paris. The museum displays models of ships (including a reconstruction of a Grecian galley), engravings and seascapes of St-Tropez, illustrating the town's long and glorious history, up to the 1944 Allied landings that unfortunately destroyed much of the town.

✉ montée de la Citadelle ☎ 04 94 97 06 53 🕐 Apr–Sep daily 10–12:30, 1–6:30; Oct–Mar daily 10–12:30, 1:30–5:30. Closed Nov and hols
✋ Moderate

Église de St-Tropez

St-Tropez owes its name to a Roman centurion called Torpes, martyred under Nero in AD 68. His head was buried in Pisa then his body was put in a boat with a dog and rooster who should have devoured it. Surprisingly, when the boat was washed up here, his body remained miraculously untouched.

For over 400 years, the town's most important festival – the Bravade de Saint Torpes, which takes part from 16–18 May – has been celebrated in his honour. A gilt bust of Saint Torpes and a model of his boat can be seen in the 19th-century baroque-style church, with its distinctive pink and yellow belltower.

✉ rue de l'Église 🕓 Daily

Musée de l'Annonciade

Here in this former 16th-century chapel is one of the finest collections of French late 19th- and early 20th-century paintings and bronzes. At that time, St-Tropez was an extremely active centre for the artistic avant-garde and, as a result, most of the hundred or so canvases here belong to the great turn-of-the-century movements of pointillism and fauvism.

Many of the paintings portray local scenes. Be sure to seek out Paul Signac's *L'Orage* (1895), Bonnard's *Le Port de St-Tropez* (1899), Camoin's *La Place des Lices* (1925), together with works by Dufy, Derain, Matisse, Maillol and Vuillard.

✉ place Georges Grammont ☎ 04 94 17 84 10 🕓 Jun–Sep Wed–Mon 10–12, 3–7; Oct–May Wed–Mon 10–12, 2–6. Closed hols 🖐 Moderate

Place des Lices

Here is the real heart of St-Tropez, which is still very much as it looked in Camoin's La *Place des Lices* of 1925 (see previous page), lined with ancient plane trees and Bohemian cafés. Visit on Tuesday or Saturday for its colourful market, or any day to enjoy a game of boules and partake of a glass of pastis with the locals.

🚌 Shuttle buses run to the beaches in summer

Tour de Suffren

This massive defensive tower is all that remains of St-Tropez' oldest building, Château de Suffren, constructed in AD 990 by Count Guillaume I of Provence. It is named after the great 18th-century seaman, Admiral Suffren, a native of St-Tropez and one of the most influential admirals of the French fleet. A statue has been erected in his honour on the quay.

✉ place Garrezio ⓘ The tower is privately owned and houses an antique shop and occasional art exhibitions

Vieux Port (Old Port)

It is easy to see why the appealing, pastel-painted houses and crowded cafés that line the quayside have enticed visitors and inspired artists and writers for over a century.

The waterfront today is very much the place to see and be seen in St-Tropez. Try to arrive in an Aston Martin, on a Harley-Davidson, or better still in an enormous yacht, and remember to moor stern-to, to give onlookers a perfect view! It's always great fun to wander along the quayside, marvelling at luxury yachts the size of ships, and goggling at their millionaire owners tucking into langoustines on deck, served, of course, by the white-jacketed crew.

For an overview of the port and all St-Tropez, the harbour breakwater (Môle Jean-Réveille) provides excellent photo opportunities.

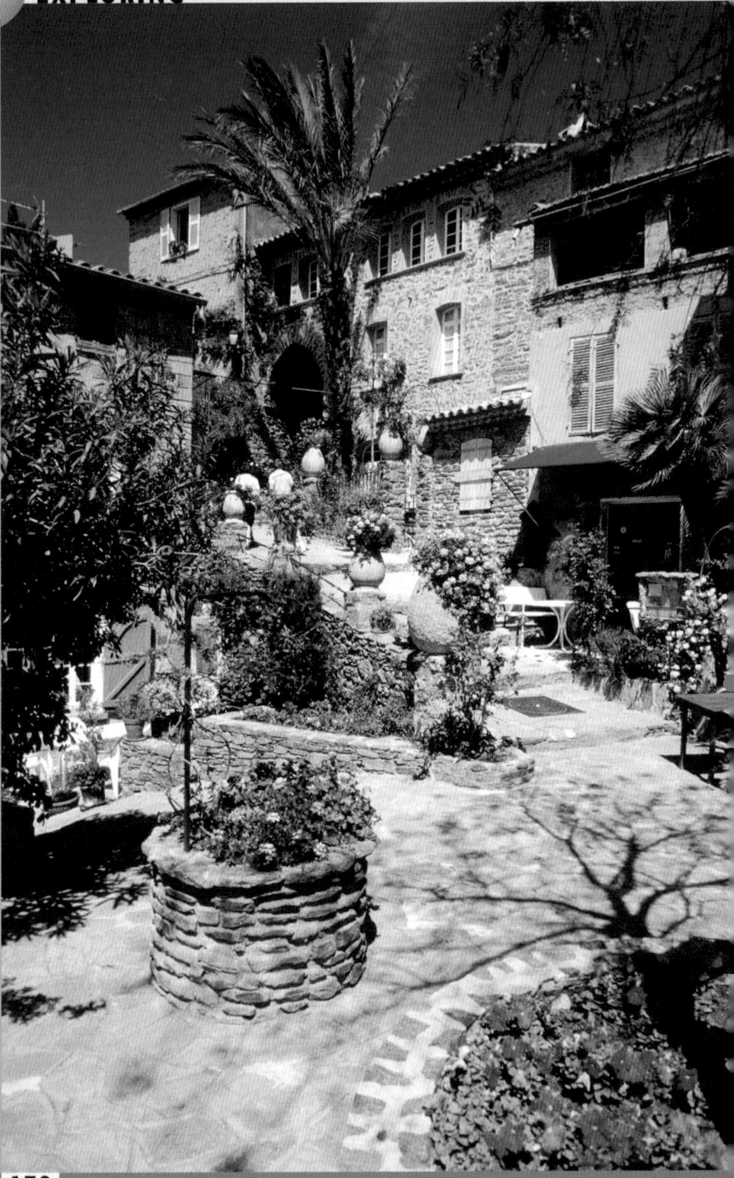

More to see on the Southwest Coast

BORMES-LES-MIMOSAS

The village of Bormes, with its ice cream-coloured houses, is undoubtedly one of the Riviera's most picturesque villages. It has had a chequered history – founded by the Gauls, conquered by the Romans, then continually sacked by Saracens, Corsairs, Moors, Genoese and finally during the Wars of Religion (1562–1598). Depending on the season, it is bathed in the scent of mimosa, eucalyptus or camomile. During February, when the mimosa is in bloom, the village celebrates with a *corso fleuri* – an extravaganza of floral floats made from thousands of yellow flowers.

A *circuit touristique* (tourist itinerary) spirals down steep stairways and alleys, with amusing names – *venelle des Amoureux* (Lovers' Lane), *draille des Bredouilles* (Gossipers' Way) and steepest of all, *rue Roumpi-Cuou* (Bottom-Breaker road)! On the way, it embraces most of the main sights, which include a fine 16th-century chapel dedicated to Bormes' patron saint, Saint François de Paule (who rescued the village from the plague in 1481), an 18th-century church built in Romanesque style, countless craft shops, and a ruined castle with dazzling views across the bay of le Lavandou and the Massif des Maures (➤ 174).
www.bormeslesmimosas.com

✚ 7C

ℹ 1 place Gambetta ☎ 04 94 01 38 38

CORNICHE DE L'ESTEREL

Best places to see ➤ 38–39.

FRÉJUS

Now merged together into a holiday conglomeration with its neighbour St-Raphaël, Fréjus lies at a strategic position at the mouth of the Argens River between the Massif des Maures and the Massif de l'Esterel. It was founded by Julius Caesar in 49 BC as

Forum Julii, an important staging post on the Aurelian Way from Rome to Arles and the oldest Roman city in Gaul. Under Augustus it soon became a flourishing naval base, second in importance only to Marseille, with around 35,000 inhabitants – a population larger than Fréjus' today.

Unfortunately, much of the Roman city was destroyed by the Saracens in the 10th century, but some vestiges remain, including sections of the walls and a tower at the western Porte des Gaules. The opposite entrance to the east, the Porte de Rome, marks the end of a 40km (25 miles) aqueduct, with a few ruined arches still visible alongside the N7. To the north, the semicircular Théâtre Romain still holds performances in summer, and to the south, remains of the Praetorium of the eastern citadel can still be seen.

Fréjus' most impressive Roman relic is the deteriorating 1st- to 2nd-century **Arène** or amphitheatre, built to seat 10,000 spectators. Although substantially damaged, it is still a popular setting for rock concerts and bullfights. During the summer months the tourist *petit train* runs between the various sites.

The town's pride and joy, however, is the 13th-century **cathedral** in the medieval town. The carved walnut doors at the entrance, dating from the Renaissance, are normally protected behind shutters. They portray scenes of a Saracen massacre and are on display only as part of a guided tour. The tour also visits the medieval cloisters, which surround a tranquil garden of scented shrubbery. Originally the cloisters were two storeys high, but only one of the upper galleries remains, held aloft by slender columns and ornately carved ceilings. The perfectly preserved octagonal baptistry is one of France's oldest.

There is also a small Musée Archéologique within the cathedral illustrating the history of Fréjus with treasures found in the surrounding countryside, including a complete Roman mosaic of a leopard and the famous double-headed bust of Hermes, discovered in 1970 (in fact a copy, as the priceless Hellenistic original is kept securely under lock and key).

www.frejus.fr

➕ 10F

ℹ️ 325 rue Jean-Jaurès ☎ 04 94 51 83 83

Arène de Fréjus

✉️ rue Vadon ☎ 04 94 51 34 31 🕐 May–Oct Tue–Sun 9:30–12:30, 2–5. Closed hols ✋ Free

Cathédrale

✉️ place Formigé 🕐 Baptistry: Oct–May daily 9–12, 2–5; Jun–Sep daily 9–6:30. Cathedral: daily 9–12, 2:30–6:30 ✋ Cathedral: free. Cloisters and baptistry: moderate ❓ Guided tours

FRÉJUS-PLAGE

Following the decline of the Roman Empire, Fréjus' port lost its significance and became silted up, forming the fine sandy beach of Fréjus Plage, 2km (1.2miles) from the town centre – a modern resort which merges into its eastern neighbour, St-Raphaël. The development of holiday homes, shops, bars and restaurants along the seafront has made Fréjus-Plage a particularly popular resort for families, thanks to its clean (albeit crowded) beach, its safe swimming and its proximity to the nearby attractions of Aqualand (➤ 74) and the Zoo-Safari-Park (next to the A8).

➕ 10F

GRIMAUD

Grimaud is one of Provence's most photogenic hilltop village, crowned by a romantic 11th-century château belonging to the Grimaldi family, after whom the village is named. Hidden amid flower-filled streets and shaded squares, you will find a beautiful Romanesque church (Église St-Michel), a restored 12th-century mill and, in the arcaded rue des Templiers, a Hospice of the Knights Templars. From the château there are impressive views over Port-Grimaud (➤ 175) and the Gulf of St-Tropez, and inland across the Maures.

www.grimaud-provence.com

✚ 8D

ℹ 1 boulevard des Aliziers ☎ 04 94 55 43 83

MASSIF DES MAURES

Just inland from the coast, the Maures mountains offer a welcome escape from nearby St-Tropez. The name comes from the Greek *amauros*, meaning dark or sombre, and it is a surprisingly unfrequented region of low hills, clothed in dense forests. Take time to explore and you will find its deserted, winding roads of seemingly endless woodland are interrupted by the occasional yellow splash of mimosa or a quaint hidden village.

Tranquil **Collobrières** lies alongside the River Collobrier at the heart of the wild Massif. In addition to cork production this village's other main industry is *marrons glacés*.

Cogolin is one of the main towns of the Maures. Its economy depends on the traditional crafts of cane furniture, silk yarn, brier pipes, knotted wool carpets and, above all, renown reeds for wind instruments. The Old Town is graced with brightly coloured houses, narrow cobbled streets and peaceful *placettes* (tiny squares).

www.collobrieres.fr

✚ 6C–8E

Collobrières

✚ 6D ℹ boulevard Charles-Caminat ☎ 04 94 48 08 00

Cogolin

✚ 8D ☎ www.cogolin-provence.com

ℹ place de la République ☎ 04 94 55 01 10

PORT-GRIMAUD

Port-Grimaud is the ultimate property development on the Riviera – a modern mini-Venice of pastel-coloured designer villas on a series of islets, divided by canals and linked by shaded squares and neat bridges. This 'film-set' village, the brainchild of François Spoerry, was built in 1968, and has since become one of France's major tourist attractions. Prices for the 2,500 canalside houses are absurdly high, but after all they're just up the road from St-Tropez. Many residents, including Joan Collins, simply jet in for their summer holidays.

The whole port is traffic-free and best explored by water-taxi (*coche d'eau*). At the centre of the village, on its own islet, the pseudo-Romanesque church of St-François-d'Assise contains stained glass by Hungarian-born Victor Vasarély and provides a sweeping view of the port from the top of its tower.

www.grimaud-provence.com

✚ 9D ❓ Tourist train links Port-Grimaud to Grimaud

ℹ 1 boulevard des Aliziers, Grimaud ☎ 04 94 55 43 83

STE-MAXIME

Ste-Maxime, with its palm-lined
promenade, its golden sandy
beach, top water sports facilities,
vibrant nightlife and popular
casino, is the Riviera's archetypal family resort. Admittedly, it lacks
the glamour of neighbouring St-Tropez, but it does provide a boat
service for star-struck tourists wishing to cross the bay and, in
exchange, it welcomes St-Tropez' overflow of visitors to its glut of
hotels and restaurants.

www.ste-maxime.com

🕂 9D

🛈 1 promenade Simon-Lorière ☎ 04 94 55 75 55

ST-RAPHAËL

Napoléon put St-Raphaël on the map when he landed here on his
return from Egypt in 1799. It developed into a fashionable seaside

resort in the 19th century. Unfortunately many of the grand belle
époque hotels were destroyed during World War II but it still
remains popular with families, largely due to its sandy beach.
www.saint-raphael.com

✠ 10F

🛈 rue Waldeck Rousseau ☎ 04 94
19 52 52

ST-TROPEZ PENINSULA

Just a short distance inland
from St-Tropez lies a
surprisingly undeveloped,
uncrowded peninsula
splashed with wild flowers
and vineyards.

In their midst, the ancient
hilltop village of **Gassin,** once a
Moorish stronghold, was built
as a lookout point during the
time of the Saracen invasions.
Today it is a colourful village, blessed with more than its fair share
of boutiques and restaurants thanks to its proximity to St-Tropez.

Neighbouring **Ramatuelle** was named 'God's Gift'
(Rahmatu'llah) by the Saracens and, together with Gassin, is one
of the most fashionable places in the region to own a *résidence
secondaire*. Every summer the village hosts popular jazz and
theatre festivals.

The countryside surrounding Ramatuelle is swathed in vines,
which produce some of Provence's most coveted wines. On the
road (D89) between Gassin and Ramatuelle, three ancient
windmills, les Moulins de Paillas, offer memorable views of the
coast and the surrounding countryside, notably the twin peaks la
Sauvette (779m/2555ft) and Notre-Dame-des-Anges
(780m/2559ft), the highest points in the Massif des Maures. To the

south, **la Croix-Valmer** is surrounded by wild, rocky woodlands. It is said that when Emperor Constantine passed through with his troops on his way to battle in Rome to claim the Empire, he had a vision of a cross over the sea, with the words *'In hoc signo vinces'* ('In this sign you will conquer'), prophesying his conversion to Christianity, followed ultimately by all of Europe. A stone cross here commemorates the legend that gave the village it's name.

✚ 9D

Gassin and Ramatuelle

✚ 9D and 9C

ℹ place de l'Ormeau, Ramatuelle ☎ 04 98 12 64 00;
www.ramatuelle-tourisme.com

La Croix-Valmer

✚ 9C ✉ Esplanade de la Gare ☎ 04 94 55 12 12; www.lacroixvalmer.fr

HOTELS

BORMES-LES-MIMOSAS
Le Bellevue (€)

Simple family-run hotel with spectacular views over red roofs to the sparkling sea.

✉ 12 place Gambetta ☎ 04 94 71 15 15 🕐 Closed mid-Nov to mid-Jan

COGOLIN
La Maison du Monde (€€€)

This small, comfortable hotel with its friendly service is excellent value, considering its 10-km (60-mile) proximity to St-Tropez. With rooms decorated with furnishings from around the world, a shady garden and outdoor pool, it provides a welcome retreat from the crowds by the coast.

✉ 63 rue Carnot ☎ 04 94 54 77 54; www.lamaisondumonde.fr
🕐 Closed Jan–Feb

GRIMAUD
La Palmeraie (€€)

Attractive small villas (with kitchens) clustered round two swimming pools, just 3km (1.8 miles) from the beaches of St-Tropez. Excellent facilities include a restaurant, tennis courts, bar, children's playground and cars, bikes and televisions to rent.

✉ quartier La Boal ☎ 04 94 55 68 00

LE LAVANDOU
Les Roches (€€–€€€)

See pages 78–79.

STE-MAXIME
Hôtel Marie-Louise (€)

A charming hotel surrounded by mimosa, oleander and umbrella pines, a short walk from the sea and well placed to explore the Massif des Maures.

✉ hameau de Guerrevieille ☎ 04 94 96 06 05 🕐 Closed Nov–Feb

ST-TROPEZ
Byblos (€€€)

Small villas, flower gardens and neat patios are clustered around a pool, fitness centre and boutiques. In summer it is the venue for the disco Les Caves du Roy.

✉ avenue Paul Signac ☎ 04 94 56 68 00; www.byblos.com

Château de la Messardière (€€€)

St-Tropez' most luxurious hotel. Truly palatial.

✉ route de Tahiti, St-Tropez ☎ 04 94 56 76 00; www.messardiere.com
🕐 Closed Dec–Feb

La Maison Blanche (€€€)

See pages 78–79.

ST-TROPEZ PENINSULA
Le Mas de Chastelas (€€–€€€)

See pages 78–79.

La Vigne de Ramatuelle (€€€)

Chic and individual vineyard villa near St-Tropez' famous beaches and nightspots.

✉ route Croix Valmer ☎ 04 94 79 12 50; www.hotel-vignederamatuelle. com
🕐 Closed mid-Oct–Mar

Villa Marie (€€€)

See pages 78–79.

RESTAURANTS

BORMES-LES-MIMOSAS
Lou Portaou (€€)

Hidden in a picturesque corner of Bormes, this small restaurant serves a simple menu of market-fresh Provençal cuisine.

✉ 1 rue Cubert des Poètes ☎ 04 94 64 86 37 🕐 Closed Tue

FRÉJUS-PLAGE
La Bocca (€)
You won't be able to resist the delicious pizzas or mouthwatering grilled meats on offer here. Reservations recommended.

✉ 407 boulevard de la Libération ☎ 04 94 53 78 54 🕒 Closed Mon

La Moule Joyeuse (€)
Moules (mussels) with lemon, *moules* with mustard, *moules Fréjusienne* with celery, carrots and thyme…

✉ 137 boulevard de la Libération ☎ 04 94 44 25 13; www.lamoulejoyeuse.com 🕒 Closed Oct to mid-Feb

GRIMAUD
Les Santons (€€)
Classic cuisine and impeccable service in elegant surroundings. One of the region's top restaurants.

✉ route Nationale ☎ 04 94 43 21 02 🕒 Closed Tue lunch and Wed

LES ISSAMBRES
Hotel Hodeo (€€€)
One of the coast's most spectacular restaurant terraces, with exceptional seasonal, organic cuisine to match.

✉ Hôtel Villa Saint-elme, corniche des Issambres ☎ 04 94 49 52 52; www.hotel-hodeo.com

ST-RAPHAËL
Café Excelsior (€–€€)
This celebrated café opened in 1938 as France's first '*café-chantant*' (live music café). Popular for its Provençal cuisine.

✉ promenade du president René Coty ☎ 04 94 95 02 42
🕒 Daily 7am–10pm

ST-TROPEZ
La Bouillabaisse (€€)
A fish restaurant in an ancient fisherman's cottage on the beach.

✉ plage de la Bouillabaisse ☎ 04 94 97 54 00 🕒 Closed Tue pm, Wed lunch, mid-Oct to mid-Feb

Le Café (€€)

Previously called Café des Arts, this has been a favourite haunt of the see-and-be-seen brigade since the 1960s. You come for the fun, not the food.

✉ place des Lices, St-Tropez ☎ 04 94 97 02 25 🕐 Daily 8–midnight

La Citadelle (€€)

This tiny atmospheric restaurant overflows on to the street. Don't miss the scrumptious *tarte tatin*.

✉ 1 rue Aire du Chemin, St-Tropez ☎ 04 94 54 81 19

L'Eau a la Bouche (€–€€)

Simple, homey cuisine on a sunny pavement terrace in a cobbled backstreet overlooking the Chapelle de la Misericorde. Excellent value.

✉ 43 rue du Portail Neuf, St-Tropez ☎ 04 94 96 03 15

Sénéquier (€€)

You can't miss the distinctive red awnings on the waterfront, for this is one of the best-known spots in St-Tropez and a must for breakfast.

✉ quai Jean Jaurès, St-Tropez ☎ 04 94 97 08 98
🕐 Daily 7:30am– midnight

La Table du Marché (€–€€)

See pages 58–59.

Vien Dong (€€)

The food here is an excellent *mélange* of Vietnamese, Chinese and Thai, but the main attraction is that the restaurant is owned by a former Mr Universe.

✉ avenue Paul Roussel, St-Tropez ☎ 04 94 97 09 78

THÉOULE-SUR-MER

La Marine (€€)

See pages 58–59.

SHOPPING

FASHION
See also pages 72–73.

Kiwi
Fashionable yet fun swimsuits, trunks and beach towels to match for the whole family.

✉ 34 rue Allard, St-Tropez ☎ 04 94 97 42 26; www.kiwi-st-tropez.com
🕒 Mon–Sat 10–1, 2:30–6:30

Quiksilver Board-Riders Club
Even if you don't surf this store will help you look the part.

✉ 33 rue Allard, St-Tropez ☎ 04 94 97 73 22; www.quiksilver.com

Senigold
Anyone who's anyone would not be seen without their sunglasses in St-Tropez!

✉ 1 rue Misericorde, St-Tropez ☎ 04 94 97 03 91

FOOD AND DRINK
Nougat Cochet
See pages 66–67.

La Tarte Tropezienne
The tempting display of pâtisseries entices you into this small shop to try *la Tarte Tropezienne* – a light, fluffy cream cake created in 1955 according to a secret recipe.

✉ 9 boulevard Louis Blanc, St-Tropez ☎ 04 94 97 19 77; www.tarte-tropezienne.com

GIFTS AND SOUVENIRS
Aux Beaux Arts
This small gallery, tucked away in a back street of the village, specializes in enchanting watercolours of St-Tropez and the surrounding countryside.

✉ Espace des Lices, 7 boulevard Louis Blanc, St-Tropez ☎ 04 94 97 87 67

La Maison des Lices

An emporium of expensive gifts and designer furniture, with two stores packed with tempting Mediterranean products.

✉ 2 & 18 boulevard Louis Blanc, St-Tropez ☎ 04 94 97 64 64; www.la-maison-des-lices.com 🕙 Daily 10–1, 3–7

Pierre Basset

You will be spoilt for choice here at Pierre Basset as terracotta and enamelled tiles, jars, pots and vases in sunny colours fill the shelves.

✉ La Route des Plages, St-Tropez ☎ 04 98 12 60 66

ENTERTAINMENT

La Bodega de Papagayo

This restaurant-nightclub near the Old Port is a good place for a bit of celebrity spotting. If you prefer your stars to be of the celestial kind there's a terrace with great views. A mixture of club nights and live bands make this a popular nightspot.

✉ résidences du Nouveau Port, St-Tropez ☎ 04 94 79 29 50) 🕙 Open almost every night during the high season.

Les Caves du Roy

See pages 62–63.

Octave Café

This chic but intimate café, piano-bar and dance club frequently has live music during summer months, especially jazz. Visiting pop stars occasionally call in for impromptu gigs.

✉ Place de la Garonne, St-Tropez ☎ 04 94 97 22 56 🕙 Daily 11pm-5am

VIP Room

This star-studded nightclub is the place to see and be seen.

✉ boulevard 11 November 1918, St-Tropez ☎ 04 94 97 14 70 🕙 Open nightly (weekends only in winter).

Index

Acknowledgements

The Automobile Association would like to thank the following photographers, companies and picture libraries for their assistance in the preparation of this book.

Abbreviations for the picture credits are as follows – (t) top; (b) bottom; (c) centre; (l) left; (r) right; (AA) AA World Travel Library.

4l Villefranche-sur-Mer, AA/R Strange; **4c** Airport, AA/A Baker; **4r** Jardin Exotique in Èze, AA/A Baker; **5l** Restaurant, AA/C Sawyer; **5r** Cogolin, AA/C Sawyer; **6/7** Villefranche-sur Mer, AA/R Strange; **8/9** Market, AA/C Sawyer; **10/1t** Menton, AA/C Sawyer; **10bl** Jardin Exotique in Èze, AA/A Baker; **10br** Herbes de Provence, AA/R Strange; **11c** St-Tropez, AA/C Sawyer; **11b** Cannes, AA/C Sawyer; **12bl** Restaurant, AA/C Sawyer; **12br** Sign, AA/A Baker; **12/3c** Salade niçoise, AA/E Meacher; **13t** Market, AA/C Sawyer; **13b** Seafood, AA/P Kenward; **14tl** Seafood shop, AA/C Sawyer; **14c** Olives, AA/C Sawyer; **14/5t** Cours Saleya, AA/C Sawyer; **15b** Peaches, AA/T Souter; **16/7** Cours Saleya, AA/C Sawyer; **17t** St-Tropez, AA/C Sawyer; **17b** Restaurant, AA/C Sawyer; **18** Roulette, AA/J Wyand; **19t** Boules, AA/C Sawyer; **19b** Perfume, AA/C Sawyer; **20/1** Airport, AA/A Baker; **25** Mardi Gras festival, AA; **28** Ferry, AA/C Sawyer; **30** Telephone, AA/C Sawyer; **34/5** Jardin Exotique in Èze, AA/A Baker; **36/7** Casino in Monte-Carlo, AA/A Baker; **37** Casino in Monte-Carlo, AA/C Sawyer; **38/9** Corniche d' Or, AA/C Sawyer; **39** Massif de l'Esterel, AA/A Baker; **40/1** Èze, AA/A Baker; **41t** Èze, AA/A Baker; **41b** Èze, AA/A Baker; **42** Fondation Maeght, AA/C Sawyer; **42/3** Fondation Maeght, AA/C Sawyer; **44/5** Îles de Lérins; AA/C Sawyer; **46** MAMAC, AA/C Sawyer; **46/7** MAMAC, AA/C Sawyer; **48/9** Musée Matisse, AA/C Sawyer; **50/1t** Fish, AA/J Tims; **50/1b** Musée Océanographique, AA/A Baker; **52** Musée Picasso, AA/A Baker, © Succession

Sight locator index

This index relates to the maps on the covers. We have given map references to the main sights in the book. Grid references for sights located on the town plan are italicized. Some sights within towns may not be plotted on the maps.